Simplified

Multiple Offense

for

Winning Basketball

Simplified
Multiple Offense
for
Winning Basketball

Cornelius Bykerk

Parker Publishing Company, Inc. West Nyack, N.Y.

PRINTED IN THE UNITED STATES OF AMERICA
BC—0-13-810507-3

Dedication

To Wes Vryhof who served as varsity
basketball coach at Grand Rapids Central
Christian High School from 1949–1964.
Serving as his assistant for four years
proved to be an unforgettable learning experience. His approach toward the game,
the officials, and the boys he coached was
inspired by a demeanor worthy of emula-
tion.

Foreword

The late John Benington, former head basketball coach at Michigan State, held high respect for Coach Cornie Bykerk and planned to write the foreword to this book before his untimely death. This honor has been bestowed upon me and, in behalf of Coach Benington, I enthusiastically recommend this book for all high school basketball coaches—veteran and novice alike.

Coach Benington was an exponent of the balanced attack in basketball offense in which a team blends fast break and pattern, developed through repetitive and progressive drills. To play a balanced system and to successfully exploit defenses, individual initiative and the concept of operational areas must be encouraged and inculcated within the framework of the pattern. Coach Bykerk's teams have demonstrated this quality and his book provides inside information on how he accomplishes these objectives.

The Grand Rapids East Christian basketball teams of Coach Bykerk are renowned in our state of Michigan, even though the school has only been in existence a few years. His teams have been perennially highly rated in the state basketball polls despite a rigorous schedule of teams much larger in enrollment in the strong Grand Rapids conference. His teams are consistently state championship contenders and won the coveted state title in 1966.

This book is a must for the library of any coach. The team organization and individual fundamentals covered provide much useful material for all levels. The book is unique in many respects. In particular the last chapter devoted to Christian goals and perspectives gives the coach insight into the importance of the intangible derivatives of the game of basketball and coaching which are so vital in these times.

GUS GANAKAS
HEAD BASKETBALL COACH
MICHIGAN STATE UNIVERSITY

Why This Book
Can Be Important to You

Basketball is a science, and like science, it is predictive. Results vary only when execution is not consistent. The best teams distinguish themselves by doing simple things correctly and with precision.

The value of this book does not depend solely on the presentation of a tested multiple offense strategy. It places equal emphasis on the need for simplicity in providing the specifics that go with the strategy. It may be an arbitrary opinion, but I'd say winning basketball is 10% theory and 90% execution. If you'll analyze our team's record, covered in Chapter 12, you'll see no theoretical references as to what this multiple offense has accomplished for us. The results have been tangible, persuasive and, certainly from the coach's standpoint, highly gratifying.

Another advantage of this book is that you do not have to discard everything you are presently doing on offense in favor of what is presented here, particularly if what you are doing is working. Improve it, add to it, modify it if necessary, but use its full potential. Most of the techniques in this book can easily be incorporated into your present plan of attack, with only minor adjustments necessary.

Modern basketball is a constant challenge. Pressure defenses have forced coaches to become more imaginative in planning their offensive attack. If one idea doesn't work, the obvious conclusion is that you should try another. Basketball, again like science, is constantly changing. This book is aimed at updating offensive basketball. Defensive basketball was revolutionized during the past decade. The advent of pressure and combination defenses has forced many changes in offensive strategy. Multiple defenses demand no less than multiple offenses, and if you are going to win, the edge of importance must be given to the offensive side of the ledger.

Simplicity and multiplicity, combined with productive imagination, keynote this book. Modern basketball can be explosive. Give your team an offensive threat that can meet every defensive situation. This book shows you how.

CORNIE BYKERK

Contents

Key to Illustrations

◯	Offensive Man
✕	Defensive Man
⊤	Coach
⟶	Running—the Path and Direction of Movement
--⟶	Pass
∿⟶	Dribbling
⊢⊣	Screen
⊢↰	Roll and Screen
↳	Pivot
∿↳	Dribble and Pivot
· · · · ·⟩	Shot or Rebound

Simplified

Multiple Offense

for

Winning Basketball

Offensive Variation—

The Power Factor in Game Strategy

Modern offensive basketball demands variation. Look across the court and check the performance of modern defense. The defensive revolution we are passing through definitely gives the defense a multiple design. An impressive feature of the "new look" on defense is the ability of individuals, and teams collectively, to use different defensive strategy to their advantage. Meeting the challenges of multiple defenses requires no less than multiple offensive design.

The goal of the defense is not a secret—it must stop the offense from scoring. The defensive strategy employed varies depending upon the opponent and the game situation. A good defense reacts to the offense. If one defensive approach is not successful, you are obligated to change. This same principle also applies to good offensive strategy.

SOLVING DEFENSIVE PROBLEMS

I like to use the problem-solving method. At its most elementary level, basketball is a series of problems. The team that creates the biggest and greatest number of problems, while solving others, is the winner. Creating problems is the primary task of the defense. Solving problems is the challenge of the offense.

Problem solving begins with *identification*. Somebody has to identify what the opponent is doing. Identification is the primary responsibility of the coach. The coach should observe and analyze the defensive strategy so that he can interpret a counter attack for his offense. The second step in problem solving is *communication*. Once the coach has established the strategy of the defense he must communicate the problem to his team. Communication should be reciprocal. Players must also communicate their individual observations to their coach and to each other. These combined efforts help to clearly identify the defensive obstacles. *Reaction* is the final step in our problem-solving design. Reaction to what the defense is doing is very significant. The offense reacts and simultaneously attacks. The basic theory behind the problem-solving approach is simple. If one solution does not work, it is obvious that some other approach should be explored.

ADJUSTING TO GAME SITUATIONS

There are subtle and extremely valuable advantages for the team that can readily make adjustments on offense. To begin with, analyze what is involved in the whole adjustment process. The coach and every individual team member is forced to identify, communicate, and react. None of this can be accomplished without thinking. Therefore, the team that readily adjusts is also the team that is alert. The alert team always has the advantage. The real payoff is the fact that quick and precise adjustments become decisive.

The ultimate aim of adjustment is to control the game to your advantage. Clever manipulation of the defense puts the offense in charge. Whenever it is possible, the offense should keep the opponent guessing. This can best be accomplished by never allowing the defense to anticipate the next move. Don't be afraid to do the unexpected. The element of surprise is a potent offensive weapon. A cardinal rule of good offense is to force the defense away from their intended goal. Never allow the defense to control the game to their advantage. Make every possible effort to turn the element of control to your favor. Start by forcing the defense to change. Check the tempo of the game. Determine if the defense is attempting to slow down or speed up the game. Check rebounding positioning and how fast they attempt to clear the ball out and up the floor. Check the opponent's ability to transfer quickly from offense to defense. Check for every opportunity to take advantage of the defensive strategy.

The offense has two options for setting up their attack. They can beat the opponent at their own game or they must force the opponent to change. Stronger teams can afford an attempt at overpowering the opposition at their game. The weaker team, whether it be slower or smaller, has no alternative. They must force the opponent into giving them the control of the game tempo. Sometimes advantages can be equalized or possibly overcome by coercing the defense to change. Naturally the defense will choose to do most often what it can do best. By forcing a change, the offense may find weaknesses or at least force the defense to work with some less familiar approach.

EXPERIMENTING WITH MULTIPLE OFFENSE

Multiple offense is your license to creativity . . . and this is exactly what the game needs. New ideas are born each time a coach is willing to try something different. The rewards of finding new and improved solutions will far exceed your expectations. The goal of all experimentation is to improve. Any offense, no matter how productive it has been in the past, can be improved. It is not mandatory for you to discard your present offense, but you must always be willing to put it to the test. Variation will give you the opportunity to find new methods while improving on the old, familiar approach.

The challenge for creativeness in basketball is limitless. The future holds very bright prospects for change, resulting in the inevitable improvement of the game. Our challenge is tremendous. So roll up your sleeves, buckle your belt, and go to work. Aim at the stars! If you don't hit them, you'll land high anyway.

BALANCING POWER BASKETBALL

It is difficult to justify change for change's sake alone. Flexibility is pointless without control and consistency. For this reason I have always found it advantageous to begin the offense with a set attack. The set attack is designed around several basic patterns that are specific. Pattern basketball incorporates the control and consistency that is necessary to develop a disciplined attack. Patterns require exact execution. Results of patterns become highly predictable when execution is precise. Players soon develop confidence in certain maneuvers that work to their advantage. When the going gets tough, I find our players leaning on our basic patterns because they have confidence in them. This reliance is very crucial because repetition is a terrific stimulant for perfect execution. Mistakes occur in direct proportion to the pressure of the moment. In the heat of the battle the best offensive efforts are produced by players who respond naturally. Natural response is hard to define, but it is easily observed. The right move at the right time is the mark of a productive player. This drama has been repeated a thousand times in athletics. This quality of excellence, when the pressure is intense, differentiates the champion from all others.

Set patterns have their limit, too. For that reason patterns should always be accompanied by fast break possibilities. Offense is incomplete if it lacks either ingredient. Offensive variation is the *power factor* in game strategy. Offense is powerful when it has the potential to strike hard and often with different techniques. Patterns are designed to give high percentage shots at close range while the fast break aims for the quick, repeated attack. *Power on offense is a derivative of a well-planned balance between pattern and fast break basketball.* Many teams fail to get capacity performance out of their offense because they use either patterns or fast break to the exclusion of the other. This is a fatal mistake that robs the offense of its best opportunity to be master of the defense. Game control requires a powerful team that can either speed up or slow down the tempo of the game as the situation demands. A genuine multiple offense is designed to be the master of the game.

DEVELOPING ALTERNATIVES

It has been said, "There is more than one way to skin a cat." True, but as a matter of fact there are *better* and *best* methods. What is best cannot be determined until various alternatives have been explored. I have found that what is best for a given situation seldom remains constant in basketball. The willingness and ability to change is basic to the game. A prerequisite to change is the presence of alternatives. A basketball offense is not complete unless it offers alternatives. The opportunity to choose from a range of options adds dimension to any offense. The defense is at a distinct disadvantage when the offense has choice. The variation of execution will demand honest defense, because change makes it very difficult for the defense to predict results. Admittedly many people find it difficult, if not painful, to change. It is natural to rely on the familiar way of doing things. Therefore, it is imperative that coaches develop a genuine sensitivity to flexibility.

Variation is an integral part of modern offense. The variation should be designed to bring out the full potential of the available material. There are several distinct advantages in using multiple offensive strategy:

1. Multiple offense offers multiple solutions to the problems presented by the defense.
2. Variation stimulates both players and coaches to be more imaginative and productive.
3. Multiple offense challenges the defense to react in various ways.
4. A fresh approach reduces possibilities of staleness.
5. Variation induces excitement. Fans appreciate and expect dynamic basketball.

The following chapters explore and evaluate many different approaches to offense. The revolution in defensive basketball must capture our best imagination. Modern offense can and will meet the challenge of any defense.

CHAPTER SUMMARY

Many basketball coaches are utilizing multiple defenses. The best offensive confrontation of the multiple defense system is a good multiple offense system. The basic aim of offense is to create problems that the defense is incapable of handling. Difficult problems are created for the defense when the offense has a genuine multiple design. The best offense in basketball is a well balanced attack that combines the use of pattern offense with the fast break.

2

Exploiting the Defense
with a Simplified Multiple Offense

Let's face it. Your opponent is out to beat you. Your offense is put to the test each time you take the floor. All the defensive strategy mustered up by the opponent can be foiled by a team that is prepared to exploit the defense. In recent years great emphasis has been placed on playing good defense. Multiple and pressing defenses are cleverly devised to stop the offense. Offenses must learn to cope with many new and varied obstacles. Learning is a doing experience. In basketball it begins with individual effort and is climaxed by the collective interaction of all five players.

PREPARE TO EXECUTE

Offense is best judged by performance. The challenge of the game is to out-score the opponent. Scoring begins with execution. All teams have plays or maneuvers that are designed to score. Many teams even use the same, or at least similar plays; but the difference in performance is the result of execution. This is where coaching makes the big difference. The coach that wants results will expect performance.

Expectation accelerates execution. If a coach expects little, he gets little; if he expects more, he gets more; and if he expects the best, he gets the best. The attitude of the coach is extremely important. Satisfaction should not come easy. Demand perfect execution every time.

To be successful a play does not have to be complicated. In fact, simple maneuvers work the best because they are easily perfected. Demand perfect execution from the very beginning. Start with the very first pass, shot, pivot, or screen. Insist on every execution being complete. Players soon adjust to the expectation of the coach.

Repetition is a good learning tool. In the process of teaching fundamentals, the coach should repeat instructions until they are mastered. Break down each fundamental so that it can be thoroughly learned. Demonstrate the potential use of the fundamental being taught. Show each player how he can take advantage of the defense by executing his move. Then it's his turn to give it a try. First, try the maneuver without a defense. Do it again . . . and again! Correct the mistakes and repeat. The player must develop a feeling for what he is doing. A sense of purpose is important. There has to be an advantage to what he is doing, and he must see it very clearly.

Practice makes perfect. Try the maneuver against a defense. If it fails the first time, try it again. Work for success and don't be satisfied until it comes. Success seldom comes easy, but when it comes it will add poise and confidence. Once a player wins his own confidence, he is more apt to try the maneuver again. Each succeeding execution will encourage him to try more. Now he is ready to try new and different ideas.

Group Execution

The ultimate success of any offense is dependent upon the extent of execution performed by every individual on the floor. It is not difficult to understand that players execute in various ways, depending upon their natural ability. Maximum potential can only be attained when every player executes to the best of his ability every chance he gets. Basketball is a team game. Even a team with one or two exceptional players cannot afford to be remiss in the development of the lesser players. A team that fails to maximize its offensive threat is a team that is easier to defense. Therefore, it is imperative that every position on the floor be developed.

INGREDIENTS OF GOOD OFFENSE

Tough teams seize every opportunity to score. Good fortune doesn't just happen; it comes as a result of effort and good planning. Effort is primarily provided by the players, while good planning is the responsibility of the coach. In the course of planning offensive strategy, coaches most frequently rely on techniques that are most familiar. Consequently many different offensive systems are employed with varying success. In my opinion there are several universal offensive principles that should be incorporated regardless of the type of offense used. Every offense should include:

1. Weak side action (players without the ball in motion);
2. Deception;
3. Variation (multiple features);
4. Floor balance for rebounding and maneuverability;
5. Safety features for quick transition to defense.

Our basic offense begins with the pivot man playing low post on the opposite side of the ball. The forwards position themselves at the end of the free throw line extended, and the guards position themselves on the key lines extended (see Diagram 2–1). This basic lineup of personnel on the key lines and foul line facilitates adjustment on visiting courts. While gymnasiums vary in size and structure, these lines are the same dimension on all courts. This helps our players to find their bearing very quickly. This positioning also allows for maximum movement of the pivot while the forwards and guards have excellent driving opportunities.

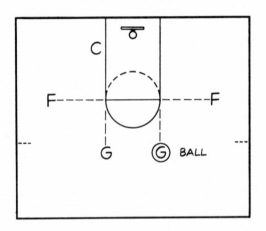

DIAGRAM 2–1
BASIC FLOOR LINEUP

There are potentially five one-on-one situations in this pattern. Each player is encouraged to make his own breaks by forcing his defensive man to commit himself. These basic positions are aimed at giving each player the opportunity to shoot disciplined shots. Disciplined shots are "high percentage" shots. Some fantastic offenses that utilize complicated plays are used by some teams. The aim of all plays is to score a basket. In our offense we eliminate the difficult plays and substitute certain patterns and techniques that will bring us the same results without being hampered by difficult maneuvers.

The five basic offensive principles listed earlier are incorporated into this offensive pattern. Many different play patterns can be used from the basic 2-2-1 or 2-3 formation. The specific patterns selected here for illustration are not significant; however, it is important to incorporate the five basic offensive principles.

Our favorite, and most productive pattern, is the inside and outside screen combination. The inside screen pattern (Diagram 2–2) begins with guard #1 passing to forward #3 on his side of the floor. Guard #1 follows his pass and sets a roll screen for the forward (#3) looking for a possible return pass. Meanwhile the weak side forward (#4) blind screens for the weak side guard (#2). The center (#5) breaks across the pivot at low range. The forward with the ball has four options: He can shoot off the screen. He can pass to either guard. He can pass to the pivot under the basket, or he can drive up the middle himself.

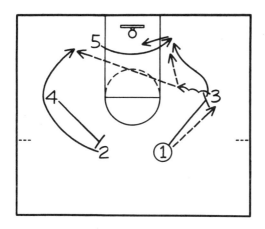

DIAGRAM 2–2
INSIDE SCREEN

The outside screen (Diagram 2–3) is used as a counter play to the inside screen pattern. Guard #1 passes the ball to his forward #3; however, he runs to the outside rather than the inside. The forward pivots and returns the ball to the guard who then dribbles to the corner. The low pivot man sets himself in a low pivot position just outside the lane. The guard in the corner passes the ball into the pivot. The strong side guard and forward tail flip off the low post. Meanwhile, the weak side forward #4 blind screens for the weak side guard #2. The pivot man has several options: He can return the ball to either man on the tail flip, shoot the ball, drive for a short shot, or pass to the weak side cutters.

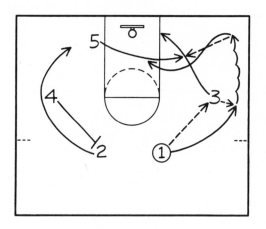

DIAGRAM 2–3
OUTSIDE SCREEN

Notice that all five players are in motion; even the players without the ball. This will force the defense into being honest all over the floor. The defense cannot afford to sag off the weakside men and gang up on the ball. Deception has been employed. The defense is never sure whether the guard will go inside or outside, or what will transpire from there. No specific results can be predicted because the offense can select from several varying alternatives, depending upon the defense applied. This flexibility is largely the result of good floor balance. Every player has a direct path to the basket and the floor is evenly occupied, eliminating congestion. The basic player positioning provides complete floor coverage for maximum rebounding opportunity. Finally, in the event the defense recovers the ball, a safety man has been designated to pick up the ball for the initial transfer to defense. This decisive transition from offense to defense is crucial. Good teams distinguish themselves by means of this quick transition.

Players should learn from and teach each other. Once they feel the success of executing a play, they begin to feel the need for each other. This combination of appropriate individual and collective execution will enable the offense to put the defense on the spot.

REACT TO THE DEFENSE

A good defense is only content when it keeps the opponent from scoring. A good offense is not satisfied until it begins to score. Point scoring begins with execution, but execution can vary, depending upon the circumstances. Initiate the attack with simple one-on-one maneuvers. Every player should be alert for scoring opportunities. A good offensive player never hesitates to put it to his man. One-on-one confrontation is basketball at its best. The forwards should drive the baseline with regularity, the pivot man should be a master of inside shots and tips, and the guards should be agile ball handlers and should develop deadly jump shots. Only when each position is a potential offensive threat does the defense have to play honest all over the court.

Players must learn to react to their individual defensive man. They should check his stance, feet placement, positioning, and reaction time. A good drill to identify defensive weaknesses and reaction skill is what we call our "reaction drill." Defenses are instructed to do one of two things: they either force the offense *inside* or *outside*. In our reaction drills (Diagrams 2–4 and 2–5) we begin by instructing the defensive man (X) to force the offensive man (O) outside or to the baseline (Diagram 2–4). The offensive man reacts by driving as close to his man as possible. The defense will attempt to keep his man from turning to the baseline toward the basket. At this point the offensive player crosses over, turns his back to his man changing dribbling hands, and drives to the basket.

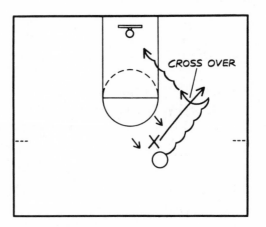

DIAGRAM 2–4
REACTION DRILL—OUTSIDE

In Diagram 2–5 the defensive man is shown forcing the offense to the center of the court. The offensive man reacts by again driving close to his man. When the defensive man moves to close the baseline, the offensive man crosses over, and drives to the basket. In either case, if the defense does not close the baseline, the offense just continues to drive for the basket. I find that players are excited by the challenge of one-on-one situations. They work doggedly to outsmart the defense. Execution like this really brings the full potential out of every player.

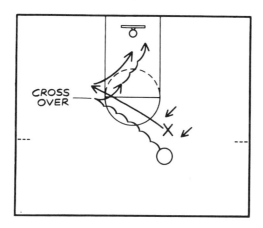

DIAGRAM 2–5
REACTION DRILL—INSIDE

Quick reaction is dependent upon identification and communication. The offense can only react when and if they identify what the defense is doing. This identification begins with each player assessing the tactics of his own man. The coach should assist and be ready to direct necessary offensive adjustments. Communication between players and the coach is essential. In preparation for a game, observations should be made of the defensive style and techniques utilized by the opponent. Pre-game briefing sessions and time outs should be used to evaluate the defense. Offense is most effective when it attacks the weaknesses of the defense.

OFFENSIVE TIPS

Begin simple by attacking one-on-one. This helps to identify individual defensive weaknesses. Look for opportunities to exploit the defense. Set screens, look for return passes, overload zones, and rebound with diligence. Execute team patterns aimed at penetrating defensive weaknesses. Work for disciplined shots that produce high percentage results. Be ready to change your attack should the defense stop your threat. Control the tempo of the game to the advantage of your offense and to the disadvantage of the defense. If the opponent wants to speed up the game, slow down the tempo. If they slow it down, you may want to speed it up. Your goal is to make the defense play at your tempo. This puts you in the driver's seat. Be alert for fast break opportunities. Score every chance you get.

A hungry offense will not leave a stone unturned in its effort to score. Look for scoring opportunities, it often is the combination of little efforts that make the big difference. Check the alignment of the defense on jump balls and during foul shots. Drive the baseline to see if the opponent is willing to give you the layup. When taking the ball out of bounds, look for passing opportunities that will lead to a score. Take the ball out of bounds quickly, and if possible, surprise the defense by sudden attack.

Finally, in judging the success of your offense, do not consider total points scored as your best indicator. A team that runs up high scores and still loses has not gained. Many coaches, in their eagerness to keep pace with modern basketball, have relied heavily on run-and-shoot tactics. By itself, fast break offense is not sufficient to meet all the challenges of really modern defense. The fast break becomes a very effective offensive weapon when it is used in combination with other offensive tactics. A team should always have alternatives to rely on when what they are doing is not effective. This combination of simplicity and multiplicity is what distinguishes good teams from all others.

CHAPTER SUMMARY

Every time a team takes the court they risk getting beat. The threat of losing, coupled with the potential thrill of winning, compels teams to execute basic fundamentals both on offense and defense. Execution is the key to success in basketball. Basketball teams are best judged by how, what, and when they execute.

Offense is incomplete unless it includes weakside action, deception, variation, floor balance, and safety features. The offensive attack becomes complete when every indivdual maximizes scoring opportunities. A potent offense blends the use of collective team patterns with selected individual moves.

3

Multiple Power Offense
with Shot Discipline

Why bother with patterns? Asking this question is like asking an army general why he bothers planning battle strategy. Patterns give offense a design, and designing offense is a *primary task* of the coach. Your teams will be evaluated most often by the quality and quantity of your scoring mechanism. It doesn't take an accomplished analyst of basketball to recognize that scoring with consistency has a distinct quality of control. This control factor is mastered by winning teams, making them capable of reproducing successful patterns time and time again.

ADVANTAGES OF USING PATTERNS

There are several distinct advantages for the coach choosing to play pattern offense. Most significant of these is the fact that the use of patterns has a way of putting the coach in the driver's seat. Patterns create expectancy! They are designed to bring about a specific set of results. The coach and his players are both aware of the potential of a given pattern. The coach is in a position to select the patterns which are most effective against the defense being applied. This control factor gives the pattern offensive team the advantage they need to win. There are many other advantages, too, including:

1. The fact that coaches may select patterns and match them with their personnel to get maximum effect.
2. Patterns give offense a higher degree of consistency which creates greater opportunities for direction and control.
3. Shots become more disciplined, resulting in higher percentage shots.
4. Patterns can be mastered for better execution and ultimate reduction of turnovers.
5. Patterns can be varied.

The ultimate success or failure of coaching cannot be determined by won and loss records. Neither can it be determined by a specific style of play, because the design of offense may vary depending upon the taste and preference of the individual coach. While the measurement of coaching is near impossible, the judging of it is very common, and on this level it can best be evaluated by the assessment of what the coach is getting out of the available material. Patterns become a coach's best friend when they are individually selected for the particular strengths of his personnel. College coaches often have the advantage of recruiting players to fit the requirements of their favorite offense. High school coaches seldom enjoy this luxury. Consequently, most high school coaches are forced to fit their patterns to their players.

Consistency—A Virtue

Patterns give offense the consistency necessary for a team to become powerful. Patterns are designed to score. They can be aimed at particular defensive weaknesses or at setting up momentary advantages for the offense. Successful patterns can be repeated. There is nothing more disheartening to a defense than to be beat repeatedly by the same move. The theory here is simple. If something works, use it until the defense adjusts or corrects itself. Then use a pattern that will beat the adjustment of the defense.

Consistency is a virtue eluding many teams, leaving them with a series of frustrations which all to often ends with defeat. Efforts at developing consistency in basketball are often frustrated by the dynamic nature of the game. Seldom are two basketball games alike, and this holds true even if the opponents are the same. All this is further complicated by the variableness of individual players, especially at the high school level. Patterns serve as a media of control, providing the coach with his best opportunity to direct the offensive attack.

Shot Discipline

Shooting is still the most important factor of offense. For this reason it deserves special emphasis. While all teams shoot the ball, all teams do not shoot the same kinds of shots. The type of shots taken will determine the level of accuracy. Shooting accuracy is affected by several factors. The most important factor affecting shooting is distance. The rule is very simple: The shorter the shot, the more accurate it is; the longer the shot, the less accurate it becomes. Therefore, shots taken from the key or within fifteen feet of the basket are higher percentage shots than those taken from further distances.

As a rule of thumb, we aim to shoot no less than 70 high percentage shots per game. If we hit 40% (making 28 out of the 70 shots taken), we will have 56 points from field goals alone. Add 15 to 20 points on free throws and your team will average over 70 points per game. Combine this offensive output with good defense and your team will be a winner.

Another important factor affecting shooting is familiarity. While basketball is essentially a team game, it still holds true that each team is made up of individuals who vary in ability and style. For this reason, each individual player develops moves which are distinctly his own. Coaches do well sometimes to overlook individual shooting differences. Correcting obvious mistakes seems proper; however, shooting mistakes unfortunately are not always as obvious as they may seem. While a certain move may seem unorthodox to the coaching eye, it may be the special ingredient making success for this boy. It is possible to over-coach. Change for change's sake alone proves nothing, and sometimes it even does harm. For purpose of analogy, consider a bowler who rolls a consistent 200 game, but who starts off the wrong foot. When he uses the correct starting foot, his average drops to 175. Would you recommend he change his starting foot?

Players distinguish themselves by developing little techniques which give them the advantage in one-on-one situations. As individuals repeat the execution of their moves, they become familiar with their own abilities, giving them the confidence necessary to successfully repeat the move again. With each repetition the move becomes more natural and more effective. Consequently, the shot at the conclusion of the offensive move is more relaxed, giving it a higher scoring potential.

I am a firm believer in the spot shooting theory. Observe your team in action. You will find players selecting certain shots over others and, as a result, scoring more consistently from some areas on the court than from others. Some players shoot particularly well from outcourt, others like the baseline, while still others shoot best with their back to the basket or at close range. Mastered patterns bring about a reflexive reaction that is highly desirable in basketball. Responses become natural and resolute. (It's almost like the response you get from a cat when it's tossed into the air. A cat always lands feet down, ready to go.) Patterns develop this type of reaction. For this reason I encourage players to find corresponding "spots" on the floor from which they most often shoot. This does not prohibit them from shooting a good shot from any place on the court, but it does encourage each player to find his best shots. Patterns can be developed to provide shots from individual spots. Meanwhile, players work on shots from their spots. These shots become familiar and, when the pattern is effective, they come at close range, giving them the best possible chance of being high percentage shots.

SHOOTING DRILLS

Chair Shooting Drill

Diagram 3–1 is the Chair Shooting Drill. Place several chairs on the court with players lined up behind them. Use one ball per chair, having each player drive up to the chair. Use the chair for a screen, and shoot a jump shot. Each player rebounds his own shot and moves to the next line. Place the chairs close to

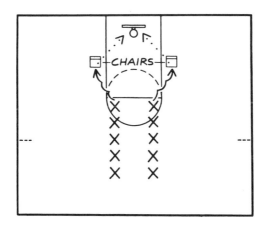

DIAGRAM 3–1
CHAIR SHOOTING DRILL

the basket at first. As accuracy increases, move the chairs back and further outside.

Timed Shooting Drill

Most shooting is done under pressure. The Timed Shooting Drill creates a pressure environment. In the Timed Shooting Drill the entire squad is paired up. The clock is set for eight minutes. One member of each group shoots while the other rebounds. Each player shoots as many shots as he can in a minute. Each player keeps count of all the shots he makes. At one-minute intervals, the shooter and rebounder switch. At the conclusion of eight minutes, each player will have shot four minutes. Tallies are made and the results are compared. The Timed Shooting Drill stimulates keen competition and arouses lots of enthusiasm. Coaches and players alike will appreciate the tangible results.

Shoot-for-Seven Drill

The Shoot-for-Seven is a competitive shooting drill (see Diagram 3–2). Divide the squad into competition groups, usually by positions (guards, forwards, and centers). On the coach's whistle, the first member in each group shoots a jump shot. The shooter rebounds his own shot. The ball is passed to the next shooter until seven shots are made by the group. This sequence is repeated at each of the eight stations shown in Diagram 3–2. At the conclusion of the drill, each group reports their results. Additional incentives can be added by administering various penalties and rewards.

MASTERING PATTERNS

I have said it before, and it bears repeating: Winning basketball is 90% execution, 10% theory. It makes little differ-

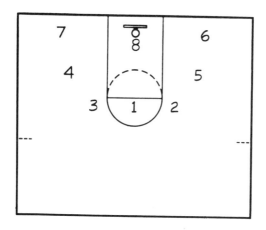

DIAGRAM 3–2
SHOOT-FOR-SEVEN DRILL

ence what a team chooses to do; it's more significant *how* they do it. The advantage of teaching patterns in basketball is that patterns are easily learned. They can be tailored to meet the needs of individual players and, finally, they become a conclusive measuring stick of performance. The sequence is clear. The coach teaches his players several patterns. Those executing the patterns the best play the most.

VARIATION

Diversion, options, multiple features . . . call it what you want, but make sure you include variation in your attack. Patterns become a tool of the coach giving him the advantage of planning the desired multiple offense effect. A planned offense enables your team to put the defense on the spot in a number of different ways.

Putting the Defense on the Spot

The aggressive offensive team will put the defense on the spot every chance it can. The defense is "on the spot" when it is confronted with a predicament. By definition a predicament is a difficult, perplexing, or trying situation. A predicament forces the defense into decision making. It is at this point, when a decision has to be made by the defense, that the offensive team has its best chance to gain control. It is also at this point that the offense is most effective if it has multiple design, because the offensive player can select his reaction and vary his approach.

Options that Force the Defense to Make Decisions

We combine the use of patterns and individual moves to put the defense on the spot. Our "Take Two" pattern is illustrative of how a pattern can be used to develop several potential predicaments and still preserve the individual opportunity to go one-on-one. Diagram 3–3 shows the basic design of the "Take Two" pattern. Guard #1 begins the play by shouting vocally "take two!" He passes the ball to the strong side forward #3 and then screens for the weak side guard #2 and continues through to screen for the weak side forward #4. Then he assumes a safety position for quick transition to defense. On the initial pass to the strong side forward, the pivot man #5 comes across the court for a potential low pivot pass. If the pivot fails to receive the ball, he returns to the weak side so that the baseline will be open for the drive. Forward #3 has three passing options: He can pass to the low pivot, to the weak side guard cutting up the middle, or to the weak side forward. If the defense plays the passing lanes, or gives any indication they are open to a one-on-one move, the forward with the ball merely puts it to his man on the baseline giving the offense a fourth and explosive option. All four options are climaxed by a potential high percentage shot (within 15 feet), but the significant factor making the pattern productive is the simple fact that the defense is being forced into making decisions.

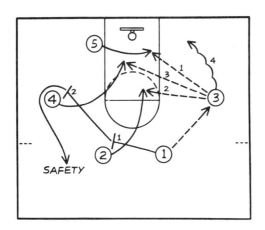

DIAGRAM 3–3
"TAKE TWO" PATTERN

Counter Patterns for Variety and Deception

A counter pattern is a complementary pattern which resembles another basic pattern but offers a completely different set of alternatives. The inside screen pattern described in Chapter 2 is a basic pattern offering several different scoring options. The outside screen pattern is a counter pattern to the inside screen. Similarly, for each basic pattern a counter pattern is developed to add variety and create deception.

The counter pattern to the "Take Two" pattern is the "Blind Side" pattern shown in Diagram 3–4. These patterns appear to be very similar, but they are distinctly different. The "Blind Side" pattern capitalizes on the sagging defense, while the "Take Two" is particularly effective against the tight man-for-man defense. In the "Blind Side," the strong side guard #1 passes to forward #3 and follows his pass around the outside to the baseline for a possible return pass. Meanwhile the low pivot man also breaks across the court toward the ball. The weak side forward #4 breaks from the blind side to the top of the key and receives a pass from forward #3. This is the prime target pass for this pattern allowing the weak side forward to either shoot a fifteen footer, drive up the middle, or pass to the low pivot under the bucket. Secondary options include possible passes to the low pivot or to the guard in the corner. Again the one-on-one potentials are unlimited.

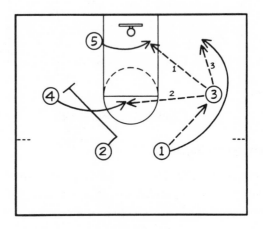

DIAGRAM 3–4
"BLIND SIDE" PATTERN

Counter patterns complement basic patterns on two levels: First, counter patterns add variety, giving more choices to the offense. This will complicate the decision making of the defense. Secondly, counter patterns add deception which compounds the uncertainty of offensive strategy. Consequently the defense cannot anticipate what is going to happen, further complicating their defensive decision making. For example, when the offensive guard passes the ball to his strong side forward, the defense has to be prepared for many different strategies. Will the guard go inside or outside? Will he "Take Two" or "Blind Side"? Will he go one-on-one? Will he shoot? If the defense anticipates a specific move, the offense adjusts by executing another move. Therefore, counter patterns give the offense multiple features which increase scoring possibilities dramatically.

OFFENSIVE STUNTING

I like to develop little stunting techniques that force the defense into unalterable predicaments. These stunts are best taught on an individual basis. This gives the coach an opportunity to get close to his boys and give little hints that are geared to individuals strengths. The results can be personally gratifying and very exciting.

Hitting the Opposite Guard

"Hitting the opposite guard" (Diagram 3–5) is one example of how a stunt can be simple, but still very productive in results. We use the "opposite guard" technique to vary our inside-outside screen patterns. The strong side guard dribbles toward the defensive man who is defensing the opposite guard. As he approaches he pivots so that his back is toward defensive man X1 and hands the ball to his teammate. The advantage for the offense after this move is subtle, but nonetheless extremely valuable. When guard #1 dribbles across court, the defense will tend to follow him. Even the defensive man on forward #3 will tend to sag off his man allowing him to get better position on the key. Better weak side positioning results for the offense when the opposite guard stunt is executed properly.

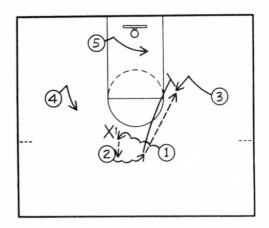

DIAGRAM 3–5
HITTING THE OPPOSITE GUARD

The Guard "Shadow" Screen

Blind screens can be employed to create havoc with the defense. Forwards can screen for guards, centers for forwards, and forwards for the pivot in single or double combinations. A favorite blind screen we use is the forward screening for the guard giving him the baseline and the screener rolling down the free shot lane to the bucket for a possible return pass or rebound (Diagram 3–6). Even if the defense calls the stunt and reacts, the offense has the advantage because they have gained position on the defense. Developing ways of getting better position is a very integral part of offensive stunting. Positioning affects ball control to the extent that it must be mastered in order to reach maximum potential on offense.

Inactivity is a big killer of offense. It is imperative for the offense to move. Continuity on offense requires that both the ball and your players keep moving. Players without the ball are most susceptible to inactivity. Check the players who are playing opposite the ball; make sure they keep the defense honest, too.

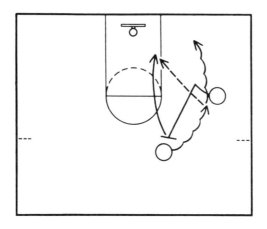

DIAGRAM 3–6
GUARD "SHADOW" SCREEN

Tail spins, sudden reverses, change-of-pace drives, pivots, and screens are stunts which can be developed individually to shake a man loose, giving him the advantage to gain position on his man.

Offensive moves should never be dead end. The task of offense is not complete until a score is made. For this reason, continuity on offense is important. Multiple features keep offense from becoming "dead end" because, if one option fails, alternatives are usually available.

Playing good offense is a full-time proposition. The attack must be relentless and continuous. Individually and collectively a good offense will never stop challenging the defense.

CHAPTER SUMMARY

Basketball is a game of momentum. The team gaining control of momentum has the edge. Patterns make the coach the captain of the offense. The control attained by employing pattern basketball provides offense with the consistency, discipline, and shot advantage that makes for winning performances.

Coaches should design patterns which force the defense into making repeated decisions. Pattern offense is capable of producing crisis upon crisis for the defense. These decisions, forced by the offense on the defense, create the effective attack capable of making the defense succumb.

4

Developing Set Patterns
for the Simplified Multiple Offense

Many coaches complain that patterns are difficult to learn, and that the complications they add to offensive design do not add commensurate scoring potential. If this is correct there is little advantage in using pattern basketball. The evidence, however, overwhelmingly supports the thesis that patterns add immeasurably to offensive potential. The best documentation to support this thesis is performance. A check of the records produced by pattern offenses settles any dispute in this area.

Begin Simply

Patterns are only as complicated as you make them. By definition a pattern is any movement that has direction and becomes a guide for repeating the execution. The direction is essential to success because it is the element that allows the pattern to be analyzed. This makes it possible for the coach to break down the pattern into basic parts. Each part is then

51

learned individually. Piecing the parts together into a multiple execution sequence, and repeating the sequence, gives any maneuver pattern status.

ATTACKING ONE-ON-ONE

Basketball offense begins, and ultimately ends, with one man challenging another for supremacy. Competition on this level is terse and intense. A good share of the one-to-one confrontation in a basketball game is unplanned. On this level players do what comes naturally, using whatever techniques they have developed for themselves. Even in these unplanned situations, the individual is limited by his personal inventory of moves. The number of choices at the disposal of the offensive man will be determined by his preparation. In modern basketball it is not sufficient to leave the development of individual moves up to the player alone. Coaching individuals involves giving them choices so they can select from alternatives which will bring the best results. Choice makes outcome uncertain, forcing the defense to play honest all the time.

Unplanned moves should be supplemented with specific tools of attack which are designed to bring specific results. The range of one-on-one moves is too massive to be left entirely unplanned. While the discovery method has many advantages in learning individual skills, there are some basic moves that should be taught to all players. Understand, these moves need not be difficult. Many of them can be learned by boys in junior high. High school basketball is placing greater demands on individual execution now than it ever has in the past. The days of throwing out the ball and expecting winning performances are over. College coaches will testify to the importance of developing maximum individual capacity. Today's basketball demands every player on the court be an offensive threat. College coaches have a keen eye for individual talent. In these days of high volume and high cost recruiting, college coaches are out to protect their investments. They want players who can do something with the ball when they get it. They also want players who can get the ball. High school coaches increasingly recognize the contribution total attack makes toward point production. They are looking for ways to improve individual output.

Begin at the level that meets the need of the individual. First, let him do what he does best. This can be determined by observing him react during free lance play. As the season progresses, I like to begin each practice session with a twenty minute one-on-one period. This allows the individual to work on his personal weaknesses. By observing others, he picks up new ideas to experiment with on his own. Whatever is learned can be tested by playing against another defensive man. The returning lettermen become valuable assistants to the coach. Their experience helps the younger ballplayers, and the pride they take in showing others how they execute their moves gives them confidence, too.

A good free lance drill for developing one-on-one skills is the Dog Fight. Line up two groups at the midcourt line, about ten feet apart. The coach has the ball at a mid-point between the two lines. The first man in each line competes to get the ball, which is passed or bounced between the two men. The drill begins as each player fights to get control of the ball. The player that gains ball control becomes the offensive player while the other man becomes the defense. Each sequence lasts for three shots or until a basket is made. If the first man to gain possession makes his first shot, the sequence is completed and the ball is returned to the coach to begin the sequence for the next two ballplayers. If he misses his first shot, both players fight for the rebound. The player who retrieves the ball becomes offense and the other man becomes defense. The drill is highly competitive, forcing players to develop one-on-one plays, and it places a high premium on rebounding skills. Scores can be tallied for each line of players, giving additional incentives.

ATTACKING THE BASELINE

The best route to the basket is down the baseline. This avenue should be continually checked. Offensive forwards and guards should repeatedly challenge the defense on the baseline. The slightest defensive opening on the baseline should be exploited. Whenever the ball appears on the baseline, regardless of the distance from the basket, the offense should test the defense in an effort to procure a baseline opening.

The baseline drill, illustrated in Diagram 4–1, sets up a one-on-one situation on the baseline. Defensive player (X) plays tough on the baseline. The coach throws the ball to the offensive player (O) who confronts the defense one-on-one, either inside or outside. Different fakes should be employed by the offensive man to gain advantageous position.

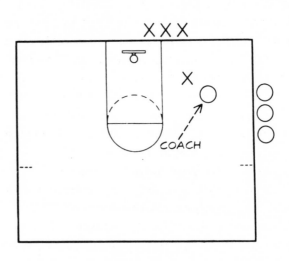

DIAGRAM 4–1
BASELINE DRILL

THE ROCKER STEP

The rocker step (see Diagram 4–2) was first developed on the college level as an individual move. At one time it was considered a complicated maneuver. This limited its use to a few outstanding ballplayers. Now it is being commonly used by high school basketball players. There are values in teaching the rocker step to all your ballplayers regardless of their abilities. Besides developing ball handling skills, each participant is given a first-hand exposure to the ideals of multiple offense, because the basic rocker step can be modified with three different adaptations.

The rocker step is easy to teach. Line up two players in a high pivot or forward position. The offensive player faces the basket with his inside foot as the pivot foot. The aim of the rocker step is to get the defense to react. Holding the ball at the outside waist, pivoting on the inside foot, and stretching as far forward as possible with the outside foot, the offensive man rocks forward. If the defensive man doesn't cover up, he makes his move to the baseline or shoots a jump shot. If the defense covers up, the offensive man rocks back by bringing his outside foot directly back. By bringing the outside foot forward again, the rocker step is continued until the offensive man catches his defensive man off blanace.

The rocker step has multiple design because it can be applied in different ways by introducing a cross-over step, a walk step, or a head and shoulder fake. All three variations begin with the basic rocker step. The cross-over is a change of direction maneuver allowing the offensive man to attack at either side of his defensive man. The cross-over develops as the offensive man comes forward on the second or later rock. As his outside foot comes forward, he cuts his stride short, momentarily planting his foot and lifting it across his inside pivot foot. The cross-over step

VISION

MOVABLE
FOOT

CHIN UP

PIVOT
FOOT
DOWN

PUSH OFF

LONG, LOW
TAKE-OFF

DIAGRAM 4–2
ROCKER STEP ILLUSTRATED

allows the offensive man to change his direction sharply and quickly.

The walk step is a change-of-pace technique. As the offensive man rocks back and forth, he breaks cadence by dragging his foot as he rocks forward. If executed properly the drag movement makes it seem like the offensive man is about to stop. If the defensive man hesitates at this point, the offensive man continues his drive.

The head and shoulder fake is designed to fool the defensive man. At the back of the rock the offensive man suddenly jerks his head and, as he comes forward, he dips his shoulders as though he is coming to a stop. Suddenly, he darts forward attacking the baseline. Hopefully, the defensive man will be taken by the head and shoulder fake, giving the offensive man a lead position.

The rocker step challenges the individual to think and to react both on offense and on defense. Encourage your players to develop their own personal adaptations to these three basic moves. In one-to-one confrontation, basketball can be exciting and highly productive.

ATTACKING TWO-ON-TWO

The importance of the individual in basketball does not diminish the fact that basketball is basically a team game. Variables are increased whenever more players are introduced into a system. The interaction of players has to be coordinated to maximize potential use of all players. Frequently two players can do what one player is not capable of doing. Two-on-two maneuvers were developed early in the game. The give-and-go or pass-and-cut were pioneering adventures in basketball. These moves gave rise to various types of screening.

Organization is necessary whenever there is more than one man playing with a single ball. Obviously two men cannot handle the same ball at the same time. One player has to give way to the other, or even better, one man can assist the other. The assistance can come in the form of a pass or screen.

There are three, basic two-man maneuvers that should be considered. The first one is the set screen. One man passes the ball to the other and then follows his pass by setting a screen as shown in Diagram 4–3. After he sets the screen, he rolls to the basket for a possible return pass.

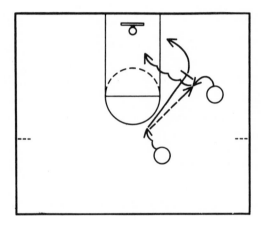

DIAGRAM 4–3
SET SCREEN

The second two-man play is the blind screen, as shown in Diagram 4–4. The forward screens the defensive man of the guard from behind. As the guard dribbles to the baseline, the screening forward fades down the free shot lane for a possible return pass.

The third two-man maneuver is a combination pivot and screen, as shown in Diagram 4–5. Guard #1 dribbles toward the defensive man of guard #2. As he approaches, he pivots and

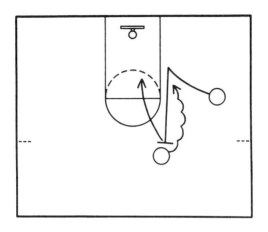

DIAGRAM 4–4
BLIND SCREEN

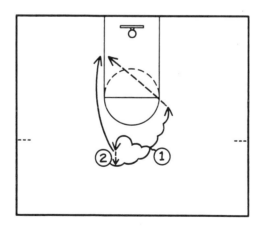

DIAGRAM 4–5
PIVOT AND SCREEN

passes the ball to guard #2, screening out the defensive man on guard #2. As guard #2 dribbles up the baseline, he looks for the opportunity to return the ball to guard #1, who breaks down the free shot lane after his screen. Even if the defensive men switch, the offensive men will have inside position, giving them a good chance to score.

The Monster Drill

The Monster Drill (Diagram 4–6) is designed to give all types of two-on-two practice both for offense and defense. The drill is set up by forming two lines under each basket, and by designating two men to be defensive men on the court. The two offensive men have to advance the ball upcourt against the two defensive men. They apply any type of offense that will give them a score. If they score, the same two defensive men cover the next two offensive men as they attack to the opposite end of the court. If the original offensive men fail to score, they play offense as long as they can retain ball possession. If the defense steals the ball or rebounds, they immediately become the offense and begin to attack upcourt while the other two members become the defense. The only way two members are relieved of being on defense is by stopping the offense or by stealing the ball. In this manner a continuous series of two-on-two situations are set up on the court. The players either learn to play defense and offense together or they suffer the consequences by running from one end of the court to the other until something gives!

Truck and Trailer Drill

Another two man drill is the Truck and Trailer Drill, Diagram 4–7, which is designed to improve pivoting and ball handling skills. The drill is set up by pairing your team into groups of two and lining the groups up at one end of the court. Four or five groups advance up the court at one time. Each group has a ball. The first player is the truck. He dribbles up-

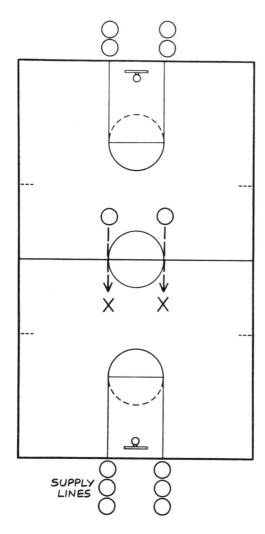

DIAGRAM 4–6
MONSTER DRILL

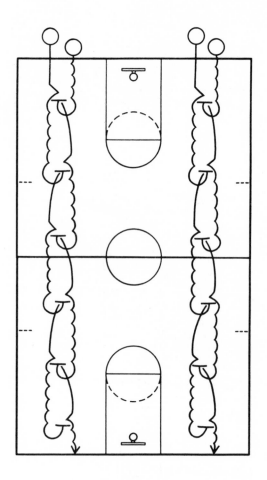

DIAGRAM 4–7
TRUCK AND TRAILER DRILL

court about five steps, pivots, and holds the ball at his waist for a handoff to the second man. The second man is the trailer. He breaks toward the truck, using a head and shoulder fake as he wipes off the truck and takes the handoff. The trailer then repeats the move of the previous truck, and the original truck becomes the trailer. This sequence is repeated to the end of the court and back again. Then the next truck and trailer take to the road.

THREE-ON-THREE MANEUVERS

Three-on-three maneuvers present broad possibilities for variation because of the increase in participants. In the progressive development of total offense this is good because each part of the offense can be represented in the form of a pivot man, a forward, and a guard. Two-on-two drills are limited to the interaction of two players, while the addition of another player increases the possibility for variation.

Many of the basic fundamental drills used by coaches are based on the use of three-man drills. The Wisconsin Criss-cross drill (commonly called the Figure Eight drill) and the tail flip drill are popular examples. The Wisconsin Criss-cross drill is so familiar that an explanation is unnecessary. In the tail flip drill a pivot man, a forward, and a guard are involved. The pivot man assumes a low pivot position opposite the ball, as shown in Diagram 4–8. The forward and the guard line up at the free shot line and lanes extended. Notice that the positioning in this drill is the same as in the basic offense patterns outlined in Chapter 3. This drill breaks down the offense into three interacting parts. The patterns developing from this drill can easily be incorporated into the regular offensive structure. In the tail flip, the guard passes the ball to the forward and follows his pass. The forward passes the ball to the pivot when he breaks to high post. Both forward and guard tail flip off the pivot, anticipating a possible return pass.

The basic formation of the tail flip can also be used for practicing parts of several other patterns, including the inside and outside screen patterns that were discussed in Chapter 2. Coordinating the play between the guard and forward, guard and pivot, or the forward and pivot can be accomplished thoroughly

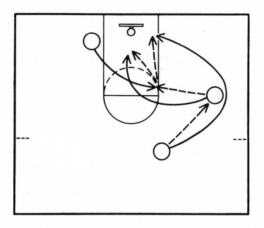

DIAGRAM 4–8
TAIL FLIP DRILL

with the tail flip drill. Among other things, emphasis can be placed on the timing of the pivot break. Blind screens can be set by the pivot and the forward. The guard and forward can both practice clear out maneuvers, and they can practice getting the ball into the pivot. One-on-one moves can be developed from all three positions. This drill also makes for good rebounding practice, with the defense forming close-out triangles on the offense.

FIVE-ON-FIVE PATTERNS

The progression from the one-on-one, to the two-on-two, the three-on-three, and finally to the five-on-five is by design. This sequence is significant because it provides for the progressive development of offense. Execution remains the key to performance on all levels of offense. It begins with individual execution, progresses to multiple execution, and concludes with team execution.

The advantage of breaking the offense into levels of execution is that various roles played by individuals in the system can be treated more intensively when separated into parts. Various types of drills and exercises are then designed to teach the basic skills of the game. The individual parts must be integrated into team patterns once they are learned. Five-on-five situations, commonly referred to as set-up time, provide a laboratory for assembling all the individual elements of offense.

I call set-up time a laboratory because this is exactly what it should be. It is the testing ground for individual and multiple execution maneuvers. The coach becomes a technician by carefully piecing the parts of offense together. Through experimentation, the offense learns its strengths and weaknesses. These strengths and weaknesses have both individual and collective character. During set-up time, the coach experiments with different player combinations. Incentives for improvement increase as players recognize their performance determines the lineup for the next ballgame. The coach's evaluation also has to include what impact the individual's contribution has on total team effort. Finally, set-up time should be used to evaluate collective performance. The ingredients of collective evaluation are discussed in Chapter 8.

The evaluation of offense is never final. Throughout the season, new techniques are added to the offensive system. The sequence of learning is progressive, developing from the simple to the complex. A typical offensive progression goes something like this:

1. Developing individual skills through the mastery of fundamentals;
2. Developing relationship skills through multiple execution drills (two-on-two and three-on-three drills);
3. Developing team patterns such as the inside screen, outside screen, take two pattern, blind side pattern, and specialty patterns.

This progression is only an example of how an offense can be developed. The specific progression may vary in content and sequence. Each year the content will change to make maximum use of the personnel available. The inside and outside screens make a good starting point because they can be incorporated into any offensive system. Specialty patterns can be drafted to capitalize on the particular skills represented by a given team. These specialty patterns serve a dual purpose. First, they provide for the maximum use of the individual skills of a particular team. Secondly, they become an opportunity to experiment with new ideas. These two ingredients make offense dynamic, and the progress they induce can be the margin of victory.

DEVELOPING BREAD 'N BUTTER PLAYS

In a sense every pattern has to be a bread and butter play. However, as the going gets tough, players will develop a dependency on certain maneuvers which best meet their needs at that specific time. The selection of maneuvers should be highly personalized so that they meet the physical traits as well as the tastes and preferences of the individual.

Every team is different. Personality differences, in combination with varying physical characteristics, give each team a distinct character of its own. During pre-season practice I take a complete inventory of the qualities of that year's team. Then I begin to sketch various patterns that will best utilize the qualities I have found. Through experimentation in practice sessions, we as a team select the patterns we like the best. Traditionally these patterns have been highly successful and they soon become real favorites for the players and fans alike.

Specialty patterns highlight a team's strongpoints. For example, a simple clearout maneuver can be developed for a strong shooting guard (see Diagram 4–9). Guard #1 dribbles to the opposite side of the court, drawing the defense along, and he passes to weak side guard #2. The forward clears out to the opposite side, teaming up with the pivot man to provide a double screen at the low pivot. The primary option of this pattern is to give guard #2 a complete side of the court to execute a one-on-one play. If a good shot fails to develop, the guard has a secondary option to pass to the weak side forward behind the double screen.

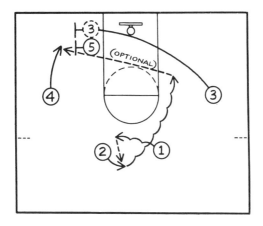

DIAGRAM 4–9
CLEAROUT PATTERN

Assume you have a tall guard that is a good ballhandler, but he doesn't shoot well from outcourt. If he has the height advantage on a guard of the opponent, you can draft a specialty pattern that will utilize his height advantage.

Diagram 4–10 illustrates the pick pattern which was designed as a tall guard pattern. Guard #1 begins the play by dribbling to the opposite side of the court. He passes to weak side guard #2 and then pivots sharply, breaking off the rear of the high post man. Guard #2 passes the ball to forward #3, who in turn passes the ball to guard #1 at a low pivot position. At the low pivot spot the height advantage pays off because even if the defense is honest, the offensive man can utilize his height to overpower his shorter defensive man. Meanwhile the pivot man screens for the weak side forward, giving the pattern an excellent release option up the middle. If forward #3 fails to get the ball to guard #1, he merely takes the secondary option and passes the ball to the weak side forward. If the defense switches men on the tall guard, the pivot is often open to receive the ball.

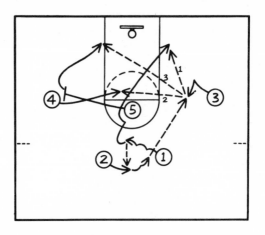

DIAGRAM 4–10
PICK PATTERN

The back door pattern (Diagram 4–11) is a variation of the pick play. Guard #1 passes the ball to his strong side forward #3. Weak side guard #2 screens his defensive man off by cutting behind the high post. As soon as guard #2 passes the post, the post man screens the weak side forward and rolls down the base line for a possible return pass. Forward #3 has the option to pass to either guard #2 or the weak side forward in the middle. If he chooses the latter, the forward in the middle has the option to shoot, pass to the pivot man, or pass to the guard under the basket.

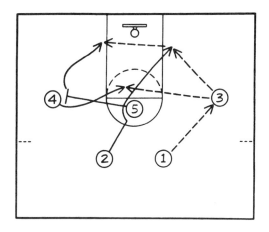

DIAGRAM 4–11
BACK DOOR PATTERN

It is delightful to make specialty patterns for good pivot men. Usually a good pivot man can play either the post or forward positions. Diagram 4–12 illustrates a combination pattern that involves both the forward and post man. Guard #1 begins the play by dribbling to the opposite side. He gives the ball to guard #2. Guard #2 returns to the strong side, passes to forward #3, and follows his pass moving through to the corner. The pivot man screens the weak side forward #4 and rolls down the base line. The weak side forward receives the ball in the freeshot lane. He has the option to shoot the ball, drive the middle, or pass to the pivot man at low post.

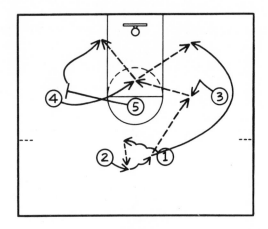

DIAGRAM 4–12
COMBINATION PATTERN

Diagram 4–13 is a transitional pattern. A team that uses both high and low pivot series should employ transitional techniques to transfer from one series to the other without wasting time or effort. Diagram 4–13 is called the Big Man Out play. Notice that the post man begins at low post, but he finishes the play at high post. This pattern begins with the strong side guard #2 passing the ball into the post man. When the ball has been received by the pivot, the strong side forward #4 breaks across the court in front of the pivot. Meanwhile guard #2 screens the defensive man of weak side guard #1. Guard #1 takes advantage of the screen and breaks around the outside of the pivot man for a possible hand off. The pivot man has several options. He can shoot, drive the middle, hand off to the guard around, or pass to the forward at low post. This pattern demonstrates the usefulness that specialty patterns have in expediting specific functions. In this case the pattern is used to transfer from low pivot to high pivot while adding scoring possibilities in the process.

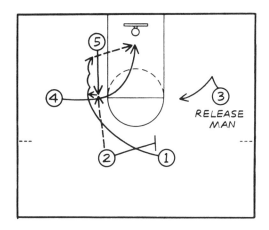

DIAGRAM 4–13
BIG MAN OUT PATTERN

PATTERNS ADD POTENTIAL

The number of combinations possible through developing specialty patterns is endless. Let your imagination run wild. Screen out the unusable parts while selecting those that work the best. Test your ideas against a defense. Then mold patterns that specifically utilize the strengths of your personnel. Players find deep satisfaction in being part of a smoothly executed play, and they quickly see the purpose in using patterns that are functional.

CHAPTER SUMMARY

The success of pattern basketball is proven by the offensive performance of the teams using it. The coach is both the architect and engineer of pattern offense. He designs patterns that capitalize on the strong qualities of his personnel.

The best offense has a simple design. Offense becomes complicated only when coaches design it that way. The beginning of good offense is one-on-one confrontation. The game is hardest fought on the one-to-one level. Each player has to use his position to challenge the defense.

The complete offensive system develops in a sequence beginning with the one-on-one and climaxing with the involvement of all five players. The offense has to be prepared to attack on the level which is probable for the moment. This could be one-on-one, two-on-two, three-on-three, any overload (two-on-one, three-on-two, four-on-three, etc.), or collectively as a whole team. Patterns add potential to the collective attack by offense.

5

Building the Best
Multiple Offensive Attack

Offensive basketball has won the fancy of player and coach alike. There is nothing more satisfying to a basketball player than to be part of a perfectly executed play. The delightful sight of watching the ball mesh through the strings arouses a feeling of accomplishment that seeks repetition.

We are living in an era of fantastic offense. The product of these new offensive efforts is higher scoring which makes for more exciting games. These high scores are not all attained by one type of offense. The route to scoring is varied. The choice of offensive style continues to grow as the inventory of basketball knowledge swells. There are many varieties of both the set-up and fast break attacks, including single post systems, double post systems, triple post systems, tandem post systems, four- or five-man weave systems, the shuffle system, or the free lance man-for-man system. Out of all these different systems the coach has to select the type of offense that best fits his team.

WHICH OFFENSE IS BEST?

Which offense is best is never constant in basketball. What may be best for one situation may not be appropriate for another situation. What is good for one team is not necessarily good for all teams. For these and other reasons the coach has to be selective in the choice of his offense.

The ingredients of good offense are detailed in Chapter 2. Coaches should consider those factors, along with the following criteria, when they select their offensive system:

1. The offense must be simple to learn.
2. It must have multiple features.
3. It has to fit your team.

A simple offense is not only easy to learn, it is easy to teach. Good coaching always is the equivalent of good teaching. Offensive tactics that are easily learned can be mastered. Then the execution of these moves becomes precise and repetitive. The execution of the offensive pattern has to be so well learned it becomes habit forming.

Multiple design gives offense the broadest potential for successful confrontation. The attack has to be waged individually and collectively. Individuals working together as a unit should employ various methods of attack. Multiple design gives offense the diversity and mobility essential to a powerful attack.

The most important criterion of good offense is suitability. The offensive design has to match up with the personnel of a team. The offensive system has to fit the playing personnel of a team like personally tailored gloves fit the hands. Here again the multiple offense offers more opportunities for the coach to select the best offense for his team. The height, speed, and playing experience of the players are determining factors in choosing the appropriate offense.

USE CREATIVE DESIGNING

Coaches have the freedom to use their imaginations in the planning of offense. There is a latent potential in every coach for producing new scoring ideas. Your practice sessions should become a laboratory where experimentation is common.

The game of basketball is in the process of being discovered. The game will continue to evolve as coaches make new efforts to improve the game. The innovations made in basketball during the past ten years have made basketball one of the favorite spectator sports in the world. There is still room for improvement, so go ahead and get started with some of your own ideas.

Begin your offensive planning by selecting basic bread 'n butter plays as a core offense. Our bread 'n butter plays are the inside screen, the outside screen, the blind side, the take two, and the pick (all detailed in previous chapters). Each year, new patterns are added to the system to exploit the talents of the new ball players.

OPTION PLAYS

Option plays, Diagrams 5–1 and 5–2, have internal multiple design allowing for several alternative scoring routes. The option play keeps the defense honest while challenging the offense to continally seek the best avenue of attack.

WEAK SIDE PLAYS

A reliable test of offense is to determine what is happening on the side of the floor opposite the ball. Weak side plays, Diagrams 5–3 and 5–4, are designed to take advantage of sloppy defense away from the ball.

CONTINUITY PLAYS

Continuity plays, Diagram 5–5, are good for offense because of the shuffling effect they create. All players move, handle the ball, and get a chance to score. The continuity pattern is not finished until the desired shot is obtained.

THE CLEAROUT SEQUENCE

The clearout maneuver (Diagram 5–6) provides the guard with one-on-one opportunities. The guard can option to drive the

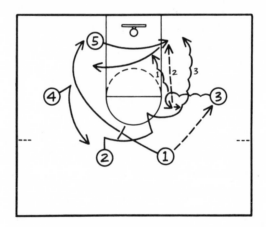

DIAGRAM 5–1

01 passes to forward 03 and screens to the opposite side for 02. 03 drives to the top of the key attempting to go all the way to the bucket. If the defense shuts off the drive, 03 pivots looking for low post 05 for option #2. Option #3 has 02 cutting off his screen for a possible handoff from 03.

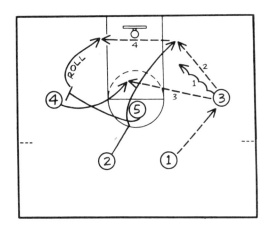

DIAGRAM 5-2

01 passes to forward 03. 03 checks to see if the baseline is open for a drive. Meanwhile 02 screens his defensive man of the high post 05 positioning himself at a low post position. If 02 fails to get the ball, he continues to the corner clearing the key for another cut by opposite forward 04. High post 05 sets a screen for opposite forward 04 and rolls to the basket for a possible release pass from either 03 or 02.

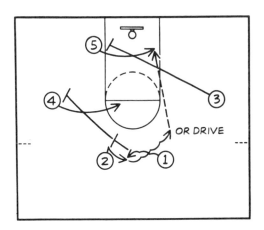

DIAGRAM 5-3

01 hands off to 02 and continues to the weak side to screen forward 04. 02 attempts to drive while looking for release passes to either 04 or 05.

baseline or open fire with a jump shot near the key. The forward and pivot men on the strong side clear one side of the floor for the guards. Screening the pivot or the forward provides excellent release routes for secondary play.

THE DOUBLE POST OFFENSE

The double post offense (Diagrams 5–7, 5–8, 5–9, and 5–10) is versatile because it presents many one on one options. It is particularly good for clearouts, baseline drives, and pivot action (high and low).

PIVOT SCREENING PLAYS

A versatile pivot man scores for the offense in many ways. Besides shooting and tipping his own shots, he has excellent floor

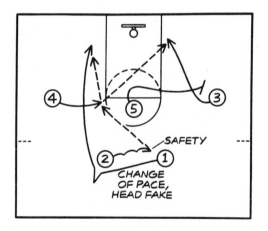

DIAGRAM 5–4

02 dribbles slowly across the court. 04 breaks to a position at the top of the key to receive a pass from 02. Meanwhile 01 has moved to the opposite side of the court for a break down the sideline. 04 can pass to either 02 or 03 who has been released by a blind screen set by post 05.

position to set screens for teammates (Diagrams 5–11 and 5–12). Screens can be set opposite the ball (weak side) or on the side of the ball (strong side).

BE SELECTIVE

Select the plays that work the best, refine them for perfect execution, and use them to their fullest potential. Most play patterns can be broken down into parts for learning purposes. Devise drills that incorporate all the basic fundamentals used in the pattern. Learn all the parts and piece them together into a working play.

Devise your own patterns, keeping your offensive system and specific player personnel in mind. Don't limit yourself to the plays in this book or any other book. Draft many different plays and select the ones that best fit your team.

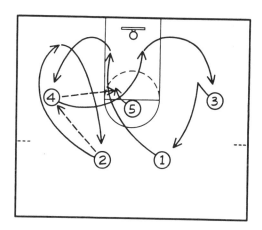

DIAGRAM 5–5

02 passes the ball to 04 and follows his pass to the corner, eventually returning to his original position. 04 passes to post 05. 01 and 04 tail flip off 05 expecting handoffs, but continuing to fill positions if no handoff develops. If no shot develops, 05 returns the ball to 03 in backcourt to begin the cycle all over again.

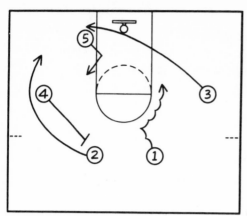

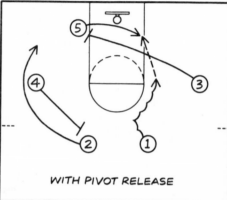

WITH PIVOT RELEASE

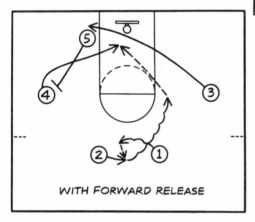

WITH FORWARD RELEASE

DIAGRAM 5–6
THE CLEAROUT

Forward 03 and pivot 05 clear out the right side of the court for guard
01. Forward 04 blind screens for 02 on the weak side.

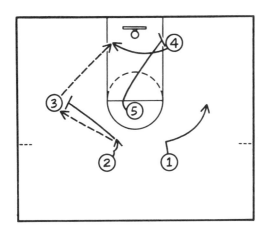

DIAGRAM 5–7
INSIDE SCREEN WITH A LOW POST CUT

O2 passes to O3 and screens for him on the inside. Meanwhile high post O5 screens for low post O4. O3 passes to O4 at the low post.

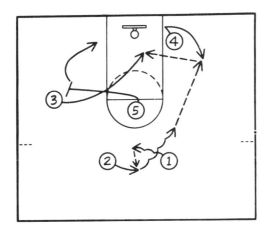

DIAGRAM 5–8
OPPOSITE SIDE SCREEN

O1 dribbles across court to move the defense, and he gives the ball to O2. O5 screens for O3 on the weak side, and he rolls to the basket. O2 passes to O4. O4 can shoot, drive the baseline, or pass to O3.

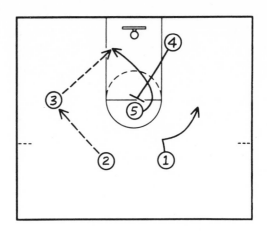

DIAGRAM 5–9
BLIND SCREEN FOR THE HIGH PIVOT

02 passes to 03. 04 blind screens for high post 05. 05 breaks to low post behind the screen looking for a pass from 03.

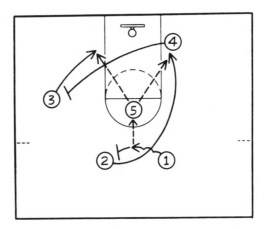

DIAGRAM 5–10
THE BACK DOOR

01 dribbles to the center of the court. He passes the ball to high post 05 and continues running to screen 02's defensive man. 04 screens for 03. 02 breaks around high post 05. 05 has the option to go one-on-one or pass to either 02 or 03.

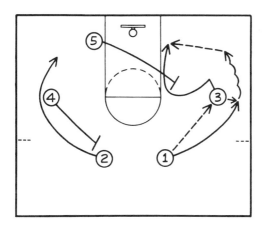

DIAGRAM 5–11
STRONG SIDE PIVOT SCREEN PLAY

01 passes to 03. He follows for a return pass. 01 tests the baseline, if the baseline is blocked he release passes to 03. 05 sets himself at the top of the key. 03 screens his defensive man off on 05 looking for a pass from 01. 04 blind screens for 02 on the weak side.

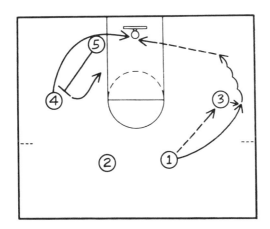

DIAGRAM 5–12
WEAK SIDE PIVOT SCREEN PLAY

01 passes to 03. He tests the baseline; if it is blocked he passes to 04 who has been screened free by 05.

83

CHAPTER SUMMARY

Variation is a prime characteristic of effective offense. The offense is never sure what type of strategy is going to be employed by the defense. Good offense retaliates by creating equal doubt for the defense. Uncertainty is the product of good offensive planning.

A broad range of alternatives is available to the imaginative coach. Select the plays that best fit your team. Demand execution of these plays on offense, but allow for individual, free lance attack whenever it is desirable.

6

Steps to Pivot Play Success
in a Simplified Multiple Offense

A good pivot man is not easy to find. He must be a jack of many trades and a master of several. If the post man is going to be pivotal to the success of the offense, he has to accomplish many things. Accomplishments never come easy when you are thrust into the center of things, and this is exactly where the pivot man will be. A good basketball center is to the offense what an axle is to the wheel—the stronger the axle, the more weight the wheels can carry. In a similar way the pivot man affects total offensive performance. The pivot, depending upon how weak or strong it is, often determines how successful the offense will be.

Developing the pivot man is not a simple task because he has so many different things to do for the offense. Failure to develop the full potential of the pivot position is a terrific waste of both manpower and prime floor space. Usually a coach screens his candidates and selects some of his better prospects to be used as pivot men. This is a wise move because the pivot man is the literal center of the offense. He enjoys the best position on the floor in relation to the basket. Naturally, for rebounding and scoring purposes, coaches will want to take advantage of this prime floor position by putting their biggest and best men there.

THE PIVOT MAN

The pivot man has to wear many different "hats." As the center of the offense he becomes a leading playmaker; because of his advantageous position he should be a leading rebounder; and hopefully he will contribute his share to the scoring. To develop a step-by-step program for training the pivot man, it is helpful to carefully analyze his work. To be comprehensive, a training plan has to consider the pivot man as a playmaker, as a scorer, as a rebounder, and as a defensive man.

The Pivot as a Playmaker

If the pivot man wants the ball his share of the time, he has to gain the confidence of his team members. There is nothing more frustrating for guards than to successfully bring the ball up the court, often against a pressing and harassing defense, only to have a clumsy pivot man muff a pinpointed pass. This doesn't happen too many times before the guards begin looking for other places to throw the ball. Admittedly, passes are seldom pinpointed, making ballhandling even more significant. As the pivot man improves his ball handling, he instills confidence not only in himself, but also in those who can potentially get the ball to him. As this confidence builds he will get the ball more often.

Procuring the ball is only part of the pivot story. What is done with the ball once it is in the pivot is even more important. The options are clear: He can pass, shoot, or drive. Selecting the appropriate alternative demands real savvy.

Setting the post is fundamental to procuring the ball. The

pivot man usually has a size advantage over others on the court. Once ball possession has been established, it is imperative for the pivot to use his body to protect the ball. There has been lengthy debate concerning the positioning of the pivot on the court. Some coaches prefer to play the pivot high post while many others use the low pivot. We use a combination by developing a high and low post series.

Techniques for shaking the defensive man have to be employed regardless of which series is used. Individuals can be taught to use tailspins, reverses, and change-of-pace tactics effectively. Balanced spacing of players on the floor facilitates these individual moves for both the pivot man and the forwards. Diagram 6–1 shows the pivot man positioned at high post. Notice that the high post position gives the forwards unobstructed baseline opportunities. Diagram 6–2 shows the pivot man in a low pivot position. The low pivot enjoys good basket position

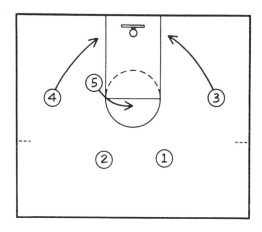

DIAGRAM 6–1
THE HIGH POST

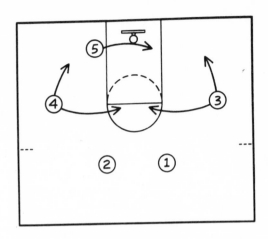

DIAGRAM 6–2
THE LOW POST

giving him high scoring possibilities. Combination techniques for freeing the pivot man are very effective.

The "swing" maneuver (Diagram 6–3) shows a forward positioning himself midway along the lane, with the pivot man swinging either in front to a high pivot position or in back to a low pivot position. The swing is designed to give the pivot man the chance to screen his defensive man off onto the forward, thereby freeing himself.

Screening is an important part of the playmaker role for the pivot man. Setting the post allows many drive off opportunities for both the guards and forwards. Perhaps the most effective screen that the pivot man can use is the blind screen. Diagram 6–4 illustrates a blind screen being set for the weak side forward with the pivot man rolling to the basket after the screen.

Screens are designed to give the offense a momentary advantage over the defense. In the area occupied by the pivot this can be extremely damaging to the defense because any mistake so close to the basket can easily lead to a score.

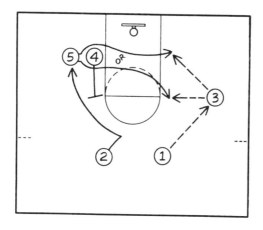

DIAGRAM 6–3
SWING PATTERN

The Pivot as a Scorer

The pivot man has the best position on the floor. Naturally he is expected to score points. Many of the points he will score will come as layup shots. Although basketball has changed dramatically in many areas, the layup shot still remains the single most important shot for the pivot man. For this reason the pivot man must be able to shoot the layup with either hand and with amazing accuracy. Many second effort shots, particularly those resulting from rebounding, are layups. The layup shot is also the climax of many drives to the bucket.

The jump shot is the second most important shot to the pivot man. The pivot man often receives the ball with his back to the basket. Therefore, he has to learn to shoot the jump shot from the position in which he most often gets the ball. As a general rule it is best to play less experienced players at low pivot positions and more experienced players at the high post; simply because the pivot man receives the ball further from the basket in

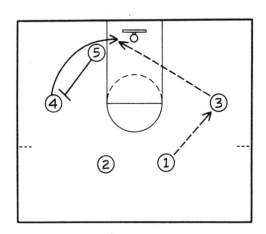

DIAGRAM 6–4
PIVOT BLIND SCREEN

the high pivot position. This means his shots and moves are at greater distances from the basket, making them more difficult. Young ballplayers do best when they first master the low pivot and then tackle the more difficult high pivot. The jump shot is effective at either the low or high pivot position.

Another shot used frequently, but not as often, is the hook shot. The hook shot is not as difficult to master as it may appear. As a matter of fact, I have found that the hook shot is easily learned if it is used at appropriate ranges. By limiting the hook shot to the low pivot position, the shot becomes more accurate and easier to learn. This shot not only adds to the repertoire of moves for the pivot, but also gives him a shot that equalizes considerable height disadvantages, adding more offensive threat.

The Pivot as a Rebounder

Rebounding is an integral part of both offense and defense. Defensively it is a sure bet because the opponent cannot score if it does not have the ball. Offensively the rebound contributes in many ways. It secures the ball for the offense and gives the offense opportunity to control the ball. It is the beginning or the end of the fast break, depending upon who controls the ball. For these and other reasons the pivot man has to become a "monster on the boards." All things being equal, the pivot man should be one of your leading rebounders. His size and floor position demand this.

Rebounding is all work and it never comes easy. There is always room for improvement because even if a team dominates the boards, seldom does it completely control. Motivating individuals, and eventually your whole team, to become real board hounds will pay handsome dividends. Stimulating your pivot man to clear the boards is half the battle. Pride is the best incentive for rebounding performance, but there are also many tangible things that can be done to develop better rebounding.

Good rebounding begins with sound physical conditioning. The size of the pivot man makes this even more significant. The entire muscular system, but particularly the leg and thigh muscles, must be extended to the fullest potential. Weight lifting, running, and jumping can all be utilized to improve rebounding skills. Competition brings the best potential out of rebounders. For this reason I like to use drills that force the rebounder to compete, thereby developing greater capacity. Diagram 6–5 illustrates a three-on-three rebounding drill, with the coach being utilized as a swing man. In this drill the players are lined up with partners of equal size. The inside men play defensively and the outside men are on offense. The coach starts the drill by passing the ball to one of the three offensive men. The offense works for the first possible open shot. As soon as a shot is taken, all six players work to get the rebound. The defensive players practice blocking out their men, forming an inside triangle. If the offense retrieves the ball, they put it back up for another shot as soon as possible. If the defense gets the ball, they clear it out to the coach and the drill begins all over.

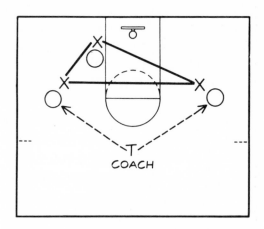

DIAGRAM 6–5
THREE-ON-THREE REBOUND DRILL

The Pivot as a Defensive Man

It has been said, "A chain is never stronger than its weakest link." This may be true in most situations; however in basketball this analogy is not always applicable. A strong defensive pivot man can compensate extensively for other weaknesses in the defense. Unfortunately it also holds true that a weak defensive pivot will compound problems. The pivot's role on defense is unique because he is positioned at the center of the defense, usually close to the basket where most of the scoring is done. This makes the pivot man the control mechanism on defense. He has the responsibility to clog the middle while guarding his own man and still remain free enough to cover up for the mistakes of others. We spend many hours of practice in overload situations, like two-on-ones or three-on-twos, giving the big men simulated game situations in which they have to protect the basket with a multiple threat developing. The pivot has to develop a sense of propriety in determining what defensive move and position would be most effective in a given situation.

SEVEN POINT DRILL TO DEVELOP THE PIVOT MAN

To be purposeful and useful, drills must have objectives. The broad objective of this drill is to develop the pivot man in every phase of his responsibility, including his roles as play-maker, scorer, rebounder, and defensive coordinator. Each part of the drill has specific goals that become apparent as the individual progresses through them. It should be understood that all of this drill may, but need not be, utilized at one time. I often use the drill in the course of a week's time, using several select parts each practice session. I always begin with the Figure 8 exercise, and then select those parts of the drill which, based on the previous game's performance, indicate need for more work.

Phase 1: The Figure 8

In the Figure 8 (Diagram 6–6), each pivot man shoots from 35–50 layup shots, alternating from the right side to the left side of the basket. If the drill is worked properly, the feet of the pivot man will follow a figure eight pattern. He should attempt to make every shot and tip those he misses right back up for a second shot.

Phase 2: Jump Shots

Begin with low pivot shots. The pivot players line up about five feet from the basket and directly in front of it. Each player takes a turn making ten shots with his feet touching the floor. This requires the shooter to exaggerate his leg and arm action. Accuracy is best when body motion is at a minimum, helping each individual to gain confidence in his shot. The next step is to

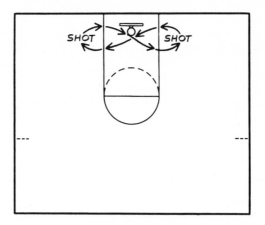

DIAGRAM 6–6
FIGURE EIGHT DRILL

shoot from the same spot, but using a jump. As players improve, they attempt the same shots at greater distances using both hands. The final phase is to begin the shot with the back to the basket. The pivot men first line up on the left baseline, while the coach assumes an outside position on the right side of the court. The coach passes the ball to each man as he approaches the spot he earlier took his standing shots from. The same procedure is used for shots taken from other spots on the floor.

Phase 3: Hook Shots

All pivot men are capable of shooting a hook shot. Begin simple, by allowing the pivot man to use the hand with which he feels most comfortable. Concentrate on short shots that produce high percentage results. This will give the pivot man the confidence he needs to be willing to use the shot. Having used the shot with success will prompt repeated use.

Phase 4: Pass Receiving

Getting the ball to the pivot often becomes a difficult task. Many defenses are specifically aimed at keeping the ball out of the pivot. Harassing tactics, double teaming, and sagging defenses are all utilized to clog the pivot. These obtacles often affect the accuracy of passes. Therefore the pivot man has to learn to handle the pass regardless of where it is. Expecting the unexpected is essential to learning in basketball.

Divide your pivot men into groups of two. One player assumes the role of the pivot man. The other man passes the ball to him, making him go after it. Vary the passes, making some high, some low, faster, slower, hooking down, over the head, below the knees, spinning, bouncing, and every place you might expect a forward or guard to pass to the pivot. Later, a defensive man can be placed on the pivot. In this situation the pass reception can be followed up by a one-on-one move.

Phase 5: High Pivot Play

It is more difficult to play high pivot than low pivot. Offensive moves develop further from the basket and there are more opportunities to drive, giving the high post unlimited potential, but making it very demanding to play. For this reason it is advisable to use the low pivot for the new and inexperienced player. When he has gained poise and confidence at the low pivot, he should be introduced to high pivot play. At the high pivot he will receive the ball with his back to the basket. Therefore, he must first learn to play with his back to the basket. Line the pivot men up at a low pivot position. Each man breaks to a high pivot position, receiving the ball from the coach or designated player who is at a guard position. The pivot man, having received the ball, practices laying the ball on the floor and making individual moves from his high post position.

Laying the ball on the floor is a very important part of any successful drive attempt. Many coaches recommend the cross-over method for initiating a drive. With the cross-over the pivot man lays the ball on the floor w:th the opposite hand of the direction he is going. For example, the pivot man receives the ball at high pivot with his back to the basket. If he determines to go to his left, he begins by placing the ball on the floor with his right hand and continues the drive. A quicker and more deceptive method for initiating the drive is to lay the ball on the court directly with the hand of the direction to be pursued. If the pivot is going to his left, he uses his left hand. This method saves a step and allows the pivot a better faking opportunity.

Phase 6: Rebounding

Anything that encourages a player to jump is good for developing rebounding. Jumping jacks, leap frog, jump rope, weight lifting, isometrics, and other leg exercises should be used continually. The retrieve drill (Diagram 6–7) is a good rebound

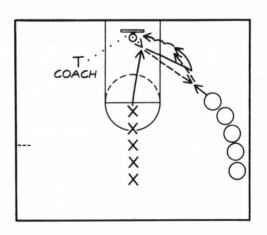

DIAGRAM 6–7
RETRIEVE DRILL

drill because it incorporates all the fundamentals of good re-bounding, including the closeout, the retrieve and the release. The retrieve drill is set up by dividing your squad into two groups. It can be limited to the pivot men, or all squad members can be included. One group lines up at the free throw line, while the other group lines up along the sideline. The coach bounces the ball off the backboard, with the first man in the middle line rebounding the ball. The ball is then released to the first man on the sideline. The rebounder follows his pass for several steps and then returns to the basket. As he returns to the basket, the ball is returned for a layup shot. The sideline man retrieves the ball to the coach and the sequence is repeated for the next two players.

Phase 7: Tipping (One-Man and Two-Man)

One-man tipping involves a single player tipping the ball up to the backboard six times and scoring on the seventh. Another alternative is to have one player overshoot intentionally, while another player on the opposite side of the basket tips the ball for the score.

Two-man tipping is more difficult because it involves competition. The competition helps to simulate game conditions, making what is learned repeatable in actual game experience. Two men are set on defense against two offensive men of near equal size. The coach bounces the ball off the backboard. The defense attempts to rebound while the offense tips whenever possible. Points can be scored for rebounds and tips, adding incentive to the drill.

THE BIG PAYOFF

There will be times when you will question if all the sweat and tears that come from exhaustive work with the pivot men is really worth the time and effort. Be patient and be assured that your work will be rewarded by improved performance. Big players often develop slowly because of their lack of coordination and timing. Usually time will produce changes which make the big difference in your attack. Be resolute and confident as you approach individual players. There is little room for doubt or negative thinking in the development of a good pivot man. Many of the attitudes of the coach are bound to "rub off" and influence the players.

CHAPTER SUMMARY

Finding a good pivot man will often go a long way toward building a strong offense. The pivot man is a playmaker, a scorer, a rebounder, and a defensive man. It takes a complete ballplayer to function adequately in all these capacities. Drills can be aimed at developing the skills required for each of these tasks. The coach has to be particularly patient with big ballplayers. Progress is often slow when working with big uncoordinated players, but the positive, reassuring approach can be extremely rewarding.

7

The Running Game
in a Simplified Multiple Offense

Speed attracts people. Kids like to run, which is good because in basketball they have to run both on offense and defense.
Fans are interested in things that move, particularly if they move
fast. Coaches teaching the fast break can appeal to this instinc-
tive desire of kids to run. As a matter of fact, kids are inclined to
go faster than they really should. Therefore, coaches often deliberately slow down the pace to make execution more accurate.
However, when the situation is ripe, never hesitate to pull out all
the stops. "Go man go" should be your motto. Whenever you
have the defense on the run, "sock it to 'em!"

The fast break is a terrific offensive weapon when it is used
properly. It adds a vital dimension to multiple offensive possibilities when it is used in combination with other offensive techniques. The possibility for complete offensive variation is dramatically increased when a team has the potential for changing
the tempo of the game.

WHEN TO RUN

Speed by itself accomplishes very little. The fast break, like any other phase of the game, must have purpose. With appropriate direction and control, it then becomes a very useful offensive weapon. A primary use of the fast break is to control the tempo of the game. Many times the offense can change the pace of the game to its advantage by running. This can be invaluable when the opponent is attempting to slow down the game. Changing the pace of the game may be vital in securing the momentum of the game. Controlling game momentum is crucial. A good offense is always sensitive to game situations. The team that keeps momentum in its favor will be the winner.

In a deficit situation the offense often has no other alternative than to run. A ten point or more spread in the later stages of a game will be fatal unless something changes. Whenever the fast break can produce several quick baskets, it may salvage the game. Several quick scores will affect game momentum. For the team that is behind, it may turn the tide. For the team ahead, it may provide the clinching blow. In down-to-the-wire situations it may be decisive. The team behind in score should always be willing to explore all avenues to change the course of the game. Deficits demand very imaginative coaching. The bigger the deficit, the harder you coach. Whenever we get more than ten points behind, I usually attempt to change the game radically. I would rather loose by a larger score if it gives us another chance at winning; even if it's only an outside chance.

The surprise attack is as old as the Indians, but it is still very effective. In these days of elaborate scouting reports, films, video taping, and television, it is not unusual for the opponent to be rather familiar with your offense. I contend it doesn't make a difference if the opponent knows what you do as long as you selectively execute with precision. The element of surprise should be built right into your offense. Earlier I stated that we usually begin our attack with set patterns. Yes, we do, but just about the time our opponent expects us to follow this course, we change. For example, we may begin the game with a few minutes of fast break . . . just enough to gain the advantage, and then settle down to our set attack. Sometimes with two or three minutes remaining in a quarter or half we may suddenly switch from our set attack to the fast break. At other times we rotate by quarters, depending upon the game situation, or even fast break for the entire game if we have the defense on the run. We will do anything within the framework of the rules which will give us the advantage or change to anything working in our favor. You can't put good fortune on like you do an overcoat. You have to make many of your own breaks. Look for opportunities to surprise the defense and convert their mistakes into quick baskets. Quickly transfer to defense and pressure the opponent into more mistakes. Be alert for opportunities to pounce on the defense. Jump balls, free shots, out of bounds situations, and sudden changes of ball possession offer excellent opportunities to surprise attack by using the fast break. Give your offense a chance to explode by using a combined punch on the opponent. Surprise attack on offense by employing the fast break and combine it with selective pressure defenses.

We want to WIN . . . the more the better! Winning teams are opportunists. They capitalize on every single opportunity to score. When the defense succumbs, the offense should strike with devastation. The fast break provides the offensive thrust to break the opponent's back once and forever.

HOW TO RUN

The quality of the running game determines its effectiveness. Unless speed has design it may do more harm than good. There are several basic principles essential to fast break success.

These principles spell the difference in performance. The mastery and execution of these fundamentals will distinguish the solid fast break attack from a sloppy unpredictive run and shoot game. This distinction is significant! The run and shoot game is not disciplined; consequently it loses a predictive quality, and tragically the offense loses the element of control. In the final analysis a run and shoot offense does not incorporate all the principles of sound offense.

The basic rules of our running game are few and uncomplicated. In sequence they are:

1. Clear the ball off the boards and out to a side court as soon as possible.
2. Then center the ball (center of floor from the sides) while filling lanes up the court.
3. Form triangles on the defense.
4. Pass whenever possible; dribble only when it is positively necessary.
5. Those following the play should fill the empty lanes. They should be alert for quick transition to defense.

These rules sound simple . . . and they are. This simplicity is important because this makes it possible to easily incorporate them into any offensive system.

The fast break begins with ball control. "You must have the ball in order to score" is an axiom that will always hold. Securing the ball involves many facets of the games. A team has to want the ball if they plan on controlling it their share of the time. Make no mistake about it, wanting the ball does not come naturally. Mental attitudes require disciplining equal to physical preparations. We actually make a conscious effort to help our players want the ball by making each player holler out "ball" after every field goal we score. This reminds each player that good defense is aimed at securing the ball. It keeps all players mentally alert for a quick transition from offense to defense. It also helps to identify the location of the ball on the court. Once the ball is located, pressures can be applied on the opponent in an attempt to force a change of possession. Change of possession occurs as a result of a turnover, after a score, or as a rebound by the defense after a missed shot. Rebounding often determines possession, and consequently it becomes a very important part of the fast break. The rebounder should clear the ball off the board and establish possession.

In the process of rebounding, the rebounder should prepare for the clearout. The clearout refers to securing the ball off the board, which is usually in a heavily congested area on the court, and passing the ball out to the sidelines where there is less congestion. As a player rebounds he should turn slightly toward the nearest sideline while he is in the air. Upon return to the floor, his body position should allow maximum vision upcourt. The ball should be cleared to a release man on the nearest sideline. Once the ball has been cleared it is ready to be advanced up the court.

We advance the ball by forming lanes up the court. The court is divided into three imaginary divisions (see Diagram 7–1), with two side courts and a middle court. There are no assigned lanes for specific players. A player merely fills the closest open lane. If all three lanes are filled, he becomes a trailer. We try to get all three lanes filled for a three-on-two situation; however, we'll take a four-on-three or two-on-one advantage, too. In any case, while the ball is being advanced up the floor, it should be centered as soon as possible. Generally the ball is cleared to either side court, but as soon as possible the ball should be returned to the center lane.

The man in the center lane is the captain of the fast break. He calls the play. He should have possession of the ball as he approaches the offensive free shot line. The player or players in the side courts attack the baseline to the basket (see Diagram 7–2). If the defense fails to pick up the center man with the ball, he has the choice of driving the middle or shooting from the free shot line. If the defense commits itself and picks up the ball in the

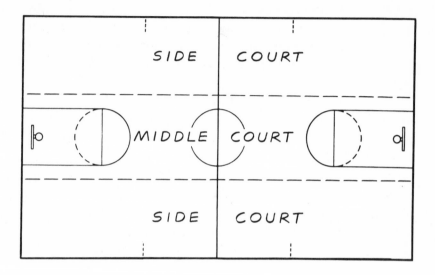

DIAGRAM 7–1
DIVIDING THE COURT FOR THE FAST BREAK

middle, the center man can pass to the open baseline man. The center man should force the defense to commit itself as soon as possible. By properly reacting to the defense, the offense will get many easy scoring opportunities. The trailers pursue the play and fill gaps that may develop in the lanes. They are also safety men on defense.

When all three lanes are filled, the offense has set up a triangle on the defense, as shown in Diagrams 7–3A and B. This triangle is the key to opening the offensive door of the fast break. In an overload situation the offense has the potential to beat the defense every time. In Diagram 7–3A the defensive center (#3) is the rebounder. He clears the ball out to the side court to a guard (#4) while the other guard (#5) fills the middle lane and the weak side forward (#2) runs the longest distance up the court.

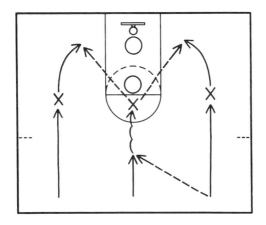

DIAGRAM 7–2
OFFENSIVE TRIANGLE

The fast break does not have to be as difficult as some coaches make it. Once kids get the "feel" for running, and master the fundamentals, they are on their way to "speedy" success.

REDUCING ERRORS THROUGH PRACTICE

Coaches must be realists when they deal with the fast break. Experienced coaches recognize there is a direct relationship between the increase in speed and the incidence of error. The faster a team moves, the more susceptible it is to error. Speed places heavy demands on execution. Therefore, if a team plans on running, it has to compensate for increased error possibilities through the mastery of fundamentals. The great equalizer is the fact that speed affects the defense as well as the offense. The method in the fast break madness is to run the defense to death,

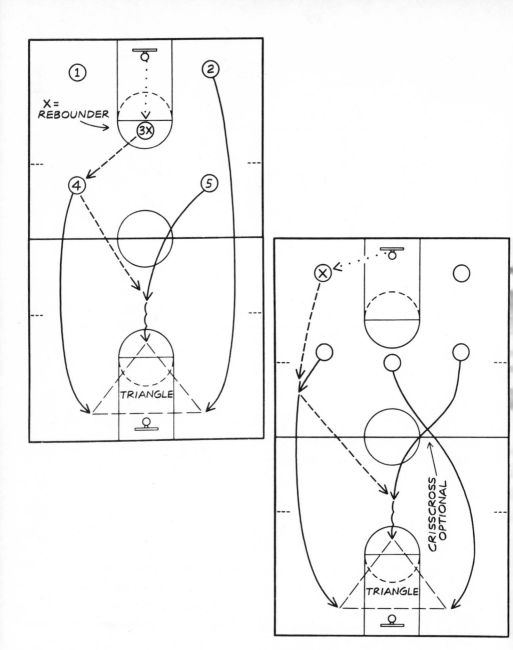

DIAGRAM 7–3A
FILLING FAST BREAK LANES FROM THE 2–1–2

DIAGRAM 7–3B
FILLING FAST BREAK LANES FROM THE 1–2–2

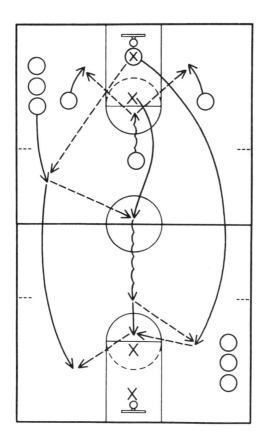

DIAGRAM 7–4
BLITZ DRILL

forcing them into repeated mistakes. Hopefully the offense will make fewer mistakes than the defense; but just hoping is not enough. Errors must be eliminated or at least reduced to a minimum. For this reason we incorporate fast break drills into our practice schedule almost every day.

The fast break drills which work the best are those simulating game conditions. I find continuity drills come the closest to presenting game conditions. Our favorite continuity drill is the "Blitz" (see Diagram 7–4). This drill develops every phase of the fast break offense. It includes rebounding, the clear-out, filling lanes, ballhandling, passing (long and short), and finally ends by setting up a triangle on the defense for the sure shot. The "Blitz" is easy to learn, kids love to run it, and it serves as an excellent conditioner because of the running factors. Set up the drill by placing two defensive men at each basket. Line up three or four men near the sidelines at both free throw lines extended. The drill begins with a group of three attacking upcourt. This sets up a three-on-two overload situation. This group continues to play until they score or until the defense rebounds. In either case, once the ball has changed possession, the two defensive men, plus the first man on the sideline, fast break to the opposite end of the court, setting up another three-on-two situation. The drill continues and players fill the defensive slots as needed.

Another popular continuity drill is the "Nut Cracker" drill. Basically the Nut Cracker is a combination of a two-on-one and three-on-two drill. Line up two men in a stack (vertical) defense (as shown in Diagram 7–5) on one court. Three men attack upcourt to create a three-on-two overload situation. These three play until they score or until the defense rebounds. When the ball changes possession, the middle offensive man (designated 2) becomes the lone defensive man. The side offensive men become the next two defensive men. The two men who were on defense fast break to the opposite basket to create a two-on-one overload situation. When the ball changes possession again, the next group of three break up the court to continue the sequence again.

Filling lanes quickly is very important to fast break success. The "Overload" drill (Diagram 7–6) develops this capacity. Although the overload is not a continuity drill, it does involve a lot of running and it is particularly good for developing outlet passes. Set up the drill by dividing your squad into a number of

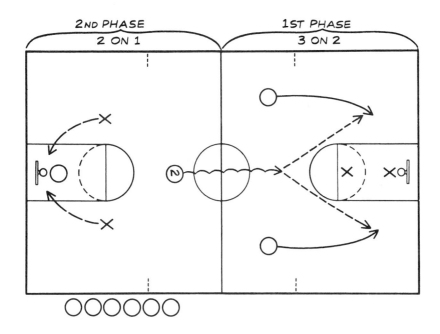

DIAGRAM 7–5
NUT CRACKER DRILL

groups, with some having four members and others with two members. Forwards and centers should comprise the groups with four, while the guards are paired together for the other groups. The drill begins with one pair of guards on offense opposing a four-man team. The guards shoot until they miss. When they miss, the defense rebounds. When the defense secures the ball, they fast break up the court. The sequence that develops is sure and simple . . . rebound, clear-out, fill lanes, pass up the court, form a triangle on the defense, and *score!* When a score is made, the teams clear the floor for the next groups of four and two. The four-man team always outnumbers the opposite team forcing an overload situation every time. The two-man team is forced to

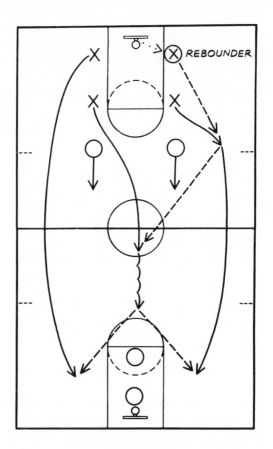

DIAGRAM 7–6
OVERLOAD DRILL

play against the overload. These circumstances often simulate game conditions for a fast break team, making the drill very effective.

A good fast break team is always a good passing team. Passing is an integral part of fast break offense. The first rule of fast break offense is to pass whenever possible. Passing accentuates speed; there isn't a faster way to move the ball. The secret to fast break success is the utilization of the one-handed baseball pass. Astute coaches always demand the two-handed passes for short-range situations, but they never fail to overlook the potential of the one-handed pass for long-range passing. When it is thrown correctly, the one-handed baseball pass is quick and can be thrown with pinpoint accuracy. It can be very effectively used as a clear-out pass or as an aerial pass to move the ball upcourt long distances. A good drill to develop the baseball pass is the "Aerial" drill (Diagram 7–7).

To set up the aerial drill, divide your squad into two equal numbered groups. Line up a group along each sideline. The drill begins by having the first man in each line dribble upcourt to make a layup. Each man retrieves his own shot, takes a dribble or two up the middle of the court, and passes to the next man who has broken upcourt. The breaking man should receive the ball just past the midcourt line and then he drives for a layup. The sequence is repeated.

CHECKING PERFORMANCE

Perhaps you have seen an effective fast break team go to work on its opponent and really tear them apart. Some teams distinguish themselves by doing this time and time again. Check their performance. You will observe that such teams are distinctive for at least five reasons:

1. They execute passes with precision.
2. They utilize pressure defenses effectively.
3. They form triangles on the defense and take delight in overloading the defense.
4. Team members work together "hand in glove," with each member anticipating the other's reaction.
5. And finally a good fast break team is always in top notch physical condition.

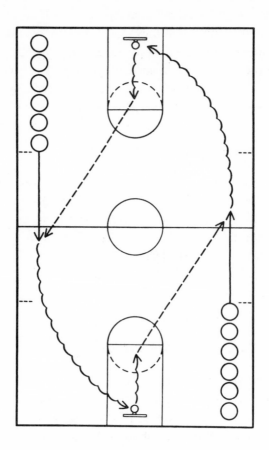

DIAGRAM 7–7
AERIAL DRILL

The best check on performance outside of real game situations is through simulation of game conditions. The Fast Break Drill combines all the skills learned in the Blitz Drill and the Overload Drill into a single continuity drill. The Fast Break Drill simulates the genuine fast break situation beginning with the rebound, clearing out to either side, centering the ball, overloading the defense, filling lanes, and setting triangles on the defense.

The Fast Break Drill involves twelve or more men stationed on the court, as shown in Diagram 7–8, with the guards at all four hashmarks and the forwards (and centers) in the lanes. The

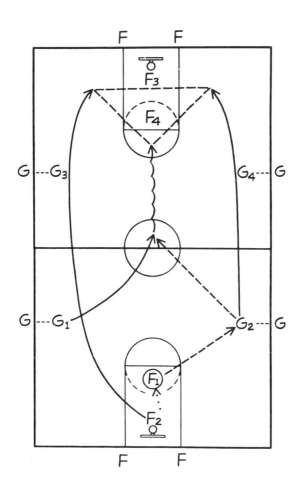

DIAGRAM 7–8
FAST BREAK DRILL

two forwards at the far basket assume a vertical stack defensive position, with one playing high post defense and the other playing low post defense. The drill begins with F1 or F2 rebounding the ball. They release a clearout pass to either G1 or G2. Appropriate lanes are filled upcourt, the ball is returned to the center of the court, and a triangle is formed on the defense. When either F3 or F4 rebounds the ball or a basket is scored, the ball is cleared out to either G3 or G4. The entire sequence is repeated at the opposite end of the court. This drill places heavy reliance upon precision passing, and precision passing is the key to success of fast break basketball.

Dynamic fast break basketball is exciting and fun to play; and more importantly, it is highly productive in modern basketball. Can you afford not to use it?

CHAPTER SUMMARY

Speed is an important ingredient of successful multiple offense. Changing the speed of offense is an effective tool. It can be used to control the tempo of the game. Like any other phase of the game, speed has to be directed to be effective. With appropriate controls, the fast break game gives offense added punch. The smart offensive team knows when to run, how to run, and what alternatives to pursue when the running game is not feasible.

The fast break introduces new pressures into the game. Some of these pressures cause problems for the defense, while others demand precision execution on the part of the offense. All phases of ballhandling including passing, dribbling, and pivoting are executed on the run, demanding more exact execution.

Without the fast break, offense is incomplete. A well oiled fast break attack gives the offense a powerful and devastating tool.

8

Getting Capacity Performances
with a Multiple Offense

The essence of coaching is to harness the combined skills represented on a team to produce capacity performances. The performance of a team is not always equal to potential. Recognizing this fact, coaches should continually assess their offensive strategy, juggle their lineups when necessary, and vary their attack to meet the challenge of the opponent with the strongest counter-attack possible. Contrary to what many fans may think, the coach usually is the first to recognize deficiencies in the offensive attack.

The limits to what can be accomplished in the counter-attack are determined by a combination of two factors. The first, and most important factor, is the quality of the material available to a coach. The only substitute for quality personnel is hard work, and even hard work has severe limitations. The second factor is an offensive system capable of meeting all the challenges presented by the opponent. Preference for a multiple offensive system of attack is logical, because it provides the offense with the range of attack necessary to meet changing defensive tactics. The evaluation of offense has to take these two factors, and the relationship between them, into consideration. The evaluation of offensive performance begins with the coach taking a complete inventory of his personnel.

TAKING INVENTORY OF YOUR PERSONNEL

The material a coach has to work with is going to be evaluated more subjectively than objectively by individual players, parents, alumni, fans, and the press. High self-evaluation on the part of individual team players can be useful if it is not done in excess. A fine line separates conceit from confidence. A player needs confidence to reach capacity performance levels. Conceit is a destructive force that robs the individual and team from ever reaching their zenith; and what is worse, it makes what has been accomplished look selfish and ugly. Players also benefit from the silent support of interested parents, alumni, and fans. The evaluations these different groups make will vary, and generally they will be inflated.

The coach also has several tools of subjective evaluation at his disposal. Admittedly, subjective evaluative criteria are always limited by the judgment-making ability of the particular coach involved; however, it can be useful if coaches play their hunches wisely. The science of coaching has progressed to the point where making judgments by the "seat of the pants" is not good enough. Effective evaluation demands a higher degree of predictability than subjective evaluation operating alone has to offer. Subjective evaluation has to be supported by the facts of objective evaluation. The individual inventory checklist should include both types of evaluation. Coaches should check each player's . . .

1. Savvy (understanding or know-how): A highly subjective criterion, but results can be measured by point pro-

duction, defensive averages, rebounding averages, assists, etc.

2. Spirit (enthusiasm or vital force): A quality that makes great impact on individual performance and team morale. This quality cannot be disguised. It is immeasurable because of its subjective nature.

3. Skills (expertness and application): Subjective by virtue of the varied standards of coaching evaluation, but objective in terms of actual contribution.

4. Speed (quickness and agility): A highly objective quality capable of being measured exactly with a watch, but it is more practically measured by observation in game-type situations. Asking the following questions gives a coach the answer: Does he beat his man to the boards? Does he beat his teammates upcourt? Does he transfer to defense quickly?

5. Size and/or spunk (comparative dimension related to determination): Notice the qualification when using size as a determinant of value. An aggressive big man in basketball is a real find; however, little men (physically) who compensate for lack of size with boundless drive and energy also make major contributions.

All five of these factors working in combination give a boy the basic ingredients he needs to be successful in basketball. Comparing these qualities in individual men can prove to be very demanding. The burden of decision making falls on the coach. His decisions should reflect complete and intensive consideration of the five basic qualities outlined above.

TAKING ADVANTAGE OF YOUR STRENGTHS

The individual inventory checklist helps a coach determine the strengths and weaknesses of his team. Isolating strengths and weaknesses is useful in two different ways: First, the coach, having identified the strengths of his team, is in a position to draft offensive strategy that best utilizes the strong qualities of his team. Secondly, a concentrated developmental program can be administered to make improvements in areas of major weakness.

The multiple offensive system provides a broad base for developing more specific methods of attack. The multiple offensive approach gives a coach a choice, as he matches the strengths of his personnel with specific methods of attack. Many variables will influence the final selection of offensive design. Height, speed, and experience are high-priority variables that often dictate specific offensive design. For example, a big, slow team can best utilize their strengths through the employment of a set system of attack. The set system will give the big, slow team ball control, while they vastly reduce turnovers with a more deliberate style of play. In contrast a small, fast team best utilizes their strengths by converting their speed into power through a fast break attack. In most cases a combination of fast break and the set attack is highly desirable because it presents the offense with genuine multiple offensive alternatives. In the final analysis, the description of the player personnel available should play a major role in determining the final mode of attack. The final attack should highlight the strong qualities of a team.

TAKING ADVANTAGE OF THE OPPONENT'S WEAKNESS

Talking about the weakness of your opponent can be extremely dangerous. Underestimating the opponent can end in tragedy. There is always the chance that he who is laughed at first, gets the last laugh. The last of the great upsets has not occurred. Underestimates of the opponent's abilities will breed damaging overconfidence. In contrast overestimating the opponent's potential can lead to defeatist attitudes, causing equal damage. The consequence of these possibilities force coaches to be diplomatic as they assess the potentials of the opponent. The description of the opponent's strengths and weaknesses cannot be ignored. Game time will bring confrontation that cannot be dodged. Appropriately dealing with the qualities of the opponent demands objective assessment, accurate non-emotional description, and meaningful application of alternatives to counterattack.

Scouting reports are intended to reveal the major strengths and weaknesses of the opponent. Pre-game practice sessions should be designed to prepare the offense to maximize scoring opportunities by countering the strengths and by exploiting the weaknesses of the opponent. Specialty patterns can be designed to capitalize on particular weaknesses that are revealed by scouting reports or previous game experiences. Here again the advantages of the multiple offensive system become abundantly clear. Offensive strategy has to vary to meet the differing qualities of various opponents. The offense offering the greatest number of alternatives is capable of handling the greatest range of obstacles presented by the opponent.

Scouting reports do not always send welcomed messages. Honest evaluation combined with realistic reporting may reveal that the opponent is likely to be stronger than your team can manage. In these situations a team has to prepare for the worst, utilizing all possible equalizing factors, and work for their best performance. The best team on paper is not always the best team on the court. Games are not decided by scouting reports, by fans in the stands, or by press writers in the press box. Games are decided on the court. Regardless of the strengths or weaknesses of your opponent, it will be advantageous to gain control of the game whenever possible by forcing the opponent to play your game.

Forcing Your Opponent to Play Your Game

The components of game control are ball possession, ball retention, and game velocity determination. Ball possession is secured by winning jump balls, by outrebounding the opponent, through recovery of the opponent's fumbles, and through successful defensive play. Once a team secures the ball, they have to retain possession until a score is made or, if stalling, until the desired time has elapsed. Reduction of turnovers is crucial to maintaining ball possession. Every turnover reduces the possibility the offense has to maintain control. Commanding the speed or tempo of the game is the final component of game control. The team that determines the velocity of the game, and maintains it at a desired level, will be in control. The desired speed will vary depending upon the strategy being employed. The control of game speed implies that the offense is capable of either speeding up or slowing down the game's tempo.

The element of game control is up for grabs throughout a basketball contest. The advantage for securing control has to go to the offensive side of the ledger, because the offense has the ball. Ball possession gives a team its best chance to become dominant. A team that has the ball can score, and conversely, a team that doesn't have the ball cannot score. What happens with the ball once it has been secured will determine the actual value of ball possession. At this point offensive execution will determine which team will secure control of the game. The multiple offensive team gains control by choosing specific methods of attack from a broad range of strategy.

SETTING THE STAGE FOR VICTORY

Good things seldom come easy; they demand hard work. In basketball there isn't a substitute for hard work. It has been said, "Luck is what happens when preparation meets opportunity." The game of basketball demands the finest type of mental alertness in a physically fit, well coordinated body. Good condition cannot be acquired in a two-week period of training before the opening of the season. The fallacy that conditioning and training are minor items and will take care of themselves, is a thing of the past. Proper conditioning is an essential part of *winning* basketball. Preparation begins long before formal practices ever begin. This is particularly true in high school basketball because most high schools have only a few weeks of pre-season practice before their first game. The coach only has a week to ten days to select his team, perhaps another week to ten days to drill on fundamentals, building up to a basic offense and defense, and a final week to prepare for the opening contest. Under circumstances like these, it is imperative for players to accept the responsibility of reporting to the first practice in "ready to go" physical condition. Some coaches require all basketball candidates who are not playing football to participate in cross country. While I encourage basketball candidates to run cross country, I don't make it a requirement. In order to enjoy and progress in cross country, a boy has to like it over a long period of time. Compelling boys to run against their will has an adverse effect on the cross country team; and many players, finding little satisfaction in their running accomplishments, lose interest and become stale. For these reasons I have developed a take-home condition program which only takes 30 minutes a day and continues for four weeks.

Our practice sessions may not begin until November 1, according to a special league adoption. Four weeks prior to November 1, I provide each varsity candidate who is not running cross country or playing football with a take-home conditioning program. Some of the big men also work on a weight training program that is specifically aimed at developing the arms and legs. The advantages of working out a conditioning program for your team are clear. The early practice sessions will reveal which players are eager to condition themselves; but more importantly, the successful conditioning program saves the coach valuable time. This saved time can be allocated to working on other important fundamentals. The players also benefit directly because their bodies are stronger, enabling them to give their best showing while attempting to make the team.

A TAKE-HOME CONDITIONING PROGRAM

FIRST WEEK

Monday

1. *Warmup exercise:* From a side stride stand (feet spread shoulders' width apart) with the arms extended from the shoulders, move the arms in circles approximately one foot in diameter, first backward 20 times, and then forward 20 times.

2. *Push-up:* Lie on floor, face down with body straight; arms bent with hands on the floor in front of the arm pits. Straighten arms and assume front leaning rest position with hands and feet touching floor.

   Counts: 1. Bend elbows lowering body until the chest barely touches the floor without taking the weight from the arms.

   2. Straighten elbow.

   Repeat 8–10 times.

3. *Trunk bender:* Starting positions: Standing at position of attention with hands straight above head.

   Counts: 1. Keep knees straight, bend over touching the knees.

   2. Knees straight, touch toes.

   3. Touch knees.

   4. Hands back above head.

   Repeat 10 times.

4. *Running in place:* Land on toes and keep knees high. Continue for 3–4 minutes.

5. *Wind sprints:* From stand still run 75 feet at full speed, walk back, and repeat as needed.

6. End session by walking around until breathing returns to normal.

Tuesday

1. *Warmup:* Same as Monday.
2. *Finger exercises:* 50 full hand grasps with hands out to either side, 50 grasps with hands extended straight out in front of the body, 50 grasps above head. Finish up by shaking hand vigorously.
3. Do 25 four count sit-ups.
4. Do 15 four count squat-thrusts (burpees)
5. Bicycle wheel for 3–4 minutes.
6. Wind sprints.
7. Walk around, breathe deeply until breathing returns to normal.

Wednesday

1. *Warmup:* Swing arms in small circles, then large circles both forward and backward. Run in place for 3–4 minutes.
2. *Pushups:* 12–15
3. *Airplane:* Starting position: Stand with feet about a foot apart; arms extended sideward at shoulder level; palms turned down.
   Counts: 1. Twist to the left and bend to touch the outside of the left foot with the right hand.
   2. Return to starting position.
   3. Twist to the right and bend to touch the outside of the right foot with the left hand.
   4. Return to starting position.
4. *Back-bender:* Starting position: Feet shoulder width apart; hands on hips.

> *Counts: 1.* Bend over and touch left foot without bending knees.
>
>   *2.* Touch floor directly in middle of legs.
>
>   *3.* Touch right foot.
>
>   *4.* Return to erect position with hands on hips. Repeat 15 times.

5. *High knee run in place:* Begin slowly and run about 15 steps (count only steps on left foot). Speed up for another 20 steps at full speed, raising knees high. Then slow down for 10 steps.
6. 8–10 wind sprints.
7. Cool down by walking around.

Thursday

1. Warm up with the finger exercise.
2. *Push-ups:* 20
3. Sit-up toe touch. Starting position: Lie on back, arms extended over head.

   > *Counts: 1.* Sit up, keeping the heels on floor and legs straight, touch your thighs.
   >
   >   *2.* Lean forward and touch toes.
   >
   >   *3.* Return to starting position.

4. *Squat-jump:* Stand with left foot about 8 inches forward, hands clasped on top of head.

   > *Counts: 1.* Sit on right heel.
   >
   >   *2.* Bounce from this position and spring forward, knees straight. Change position of feet.
   >
   >   *3.* Drop to squat on left heel.
   >
   >   *4.* Spring and change position of feet. Repeat 12 times.

5. Deep knee bends: 25
6. Wind sprints.
7. Cool down by walking around.

Friday

1. *Warm up:* Arm circles and finger exercises.
2. *Pushups:* 25
3. Four count trunk bender. 15 times.
4. Bicycle wheel for 3–4 minutes.
5. Bounce on toes 20 times reaching for the sky the last 3 times.
6. Wind sprints.
7. Cool down by walking around.

Saturday

Jog one-half mile at a moderate pace, walk until breathing returns to near normal.

SECOND WEEK

During the second week all drills of the first week are repeated in the same order, but each drill is extended to meet the needs of the individual participant. In general it is safe to assume that all exercises should be increased by half as many times during the second week.

THIRD WEEK

Monday

1. *Warm up:* Arm circles, finger exercises, and running in place.
2. Bounce on toes 20 times reaching for the sky the last 3 times.
3. *Pushups:* as many as you can do.
4. *Deep knee bends:* 15

5. Coordinating exercise: Number One: The Jumping-Jack: starting position: feet together, arms hanging at sides.

   Count: 1. Jump to wide stride, swinging the arms sideward and upward to clap the hands overhead.
   2. Jump feet together, bringing the arms to sides.
   3. Same as count 1.
   4. Same as count 2.
   Repeat 25 times.

6. Wind sprints: (50 yds.) 10–15
7. Walk it out.

NOTE: During the next two weeks our exercises will be aimed at coordinating various muscle groups. These coordinating exercises are generally a little more difficult, but now that our muscles are loosened up after two weeks of exercise, the exercises should be comparatively easy.

Tuesday

1. *Warm up:* Arm circles, finger exercises, and running in place.
2. *Four count trunk bender:* See First Week, *Monday,* Item #3, for directions.
3. Duck walk for 100 feet.
4. *Push ups:* Don't be afraid to expend yourself.
5. *Squat-Jump:* See First Week, *Thursday,* Item #4, for directions.
   Repeat 15 times.
6. Coordinating exercise number one. 25 times. Last ten times vary the exercise by moving legs forward and backward.
7. Wind sprints.
8. Walk it out.

Wednesday

1. *Warm up:* Arm circles, finger exercises, and running in place.
2. Push ups.
3. *Back bender exercise:* See First Week, *Wednesday,* Item #4 for directions. Repeat 15 times.
4. Bounce on toes 20 times reaching for the sky the last 3 times.
5. Coordinating exercise number 1, 10 times, variation of foot movement 5 times.
6. Coordinating exercise number 2. Starting position: feet together, arms hanging at side.
   Counts: 1. Spread feet and bring arms up even with the shoulders.
   2. Bring feet together, and return arms to side.
   3. Spread feet, but this time extend arms forward in front of the body.
   4. Bring feet back together, and return arms to the side.
7. Wind sprints.
8. Walk it out.

Thursday

1. *Warm up:* Arm circles, finger exercises, and running in place.
2. Push ups.
3. *Sit ups:* as many as you can do.
4. Coordinating exercise number 1 and its variation 15 times.
5. Coordinating exercise number 2. 15 times.
6. Coordinating exercise number 3. Starting position: Same as in other two.

Counts: 1–4. Same as in coordinating exercise number 2.
5. Spread feet and clap hands overhead.
6. Bring feet back together, and return arms to the side.
Repeat 8 times.
7. Wind sprints.
8. Walk it out.

Friday

1. *Warm up:* Arm circles, finger exercises, and running in place.
2. Push ups.
3. *Squat-jump:* See First Week, *Thursday,* Item #4, for directions.
4. Coordinating exercise number 2. 20 times.
5. Coordinating exercise number 3. 12 times.
6. Bounce on toes 20 times reaching for the sky the last 3 times.
7. Wind sprints.
8. Walk it out.

Saturday

Jog one mile at a moderate pace, walk until breathing returns to normal.

FOURTH WEEK

Same sequence as the third week but extended to meet individual needs.

The progressive design of this program makes conditioning more demanding as the days and weeks pass. The program is intentionally flexible enabling it to meet the needs of a broad range of participants. The convenience of administering the program at home during leisure time enhances the possibility of its being used.

Good conditioning requires plenty of rest. Inadequate sleep contributes more to mental and physical fatigue in basketball players than any other single factor. The amount of sleep required for proficiency in performance is a matter for each individual to decide; however, sufficient sleep should be acquired at the expense of everything else. As a general rule, it would be well to add one hour of sleep during the training program to what the individual has been used to sleeping. Players should make sure this additional hour of sleep comes before midnight. Sleeping late in the morning will make them feel drowsy.

A final bit of special advice for the real workers: It instructs them to dig up several old tennis balls and place them wherever they plan to be during the next month. They could put one in the bathroom, one in their car, one under their pillow, and one in their study or recreation room. Then every spare moment they have they are to grab the tennis ball and grasp it in their hands. Pinching the ball harder and harder, extending the muscles in their fingers and wrists. This little stunt will strengthen their arm, wrist, and finger muscles.

Good conditioning demands continuing effort to maintain and improve levels of efficiency. Once the season begins, we open practice sessions with some type of running drill and close each session by running laps. A coach should not conclude that fast break drills, and other running drills during practice, are sufficient to attain peak levels of efficiency. Readiness for game conditions will require a team to run more than is usually required during the regular drills incorporated into normal practice sessions. After a hard, two-hour practice we begin our extended conditioning program by running five speed laps, walking one recovery lap, running three moderately-paced laps, walking another recovery lap, and we finish with a hard endurance lap. The number of laps should be increased as the season progresses.

Running practice should be varied the same as other elements of practice. For variation in running, finish practice with windsprints instead of laps, by running a flight of stairs twenty to forty times, by running in reverse (backwards), or by using the Dog and Hare Drill.

The Dog and Hare Drill is an Australian pursuit race. Line up your entire squad in single file. All players run at moderate speed. At the sound of the coach's whistle, the last man passes all others and moves to the front of the file. This sequence continues until every player has passed all the other players. At the sound of three quick whistles, the race is for keeps. Every player pulls out all the stops, attempting to pass as many players as he can without being passed himself. As soon as a player has been passed, he is out of the race. The final man left is the winner. The winner starts at the beginning of the line the next time the drill is used, and at shower time he gets an extra bar of soap.

A SUPPLEMENTAL CONDITIONING PROGRAM

Attaining good physical conditioning is hard work; maintaining it requires more work. Peak levels of condition are best maintained by supplemental exercises. Regular practice drills by themselves usually do not extend players enough. The following supplemental conditioning program is used after the season begins. The first three weeks of practice, it is used daily. In later stages of the season, it can be used on an intermittent basis.

    I. *Warmup Exercises:* Players choose any five from the following list. Selections are varied each day.
        A. Arm circles (big and small; backward and forward) for one minute.
        B. Wall jumping: Mark the wall two feet above the extended hand with feet on the floor. Reach for heights above this line jumping at least fifty times.

    C. Toe touch: Players cross their feet, keeping knees stiff, and they bend to touch their toes. Repeat 20 times.

    D. Opposite elbow to knee: Feet are firm on floor shoulder width apart. Repeat 25 times.

    E. Jumping jack: 40 times.

    F. Trunk twisters: 35 times.

    G. Four count squat thrusts: 25 times.

    H. Push ups (on fingers: 10 times).

II. *Weight Training.*

    A. Arms:

        1. Pull over: Lying flat on bench, placing bar on ground, bar is lifted over head to stomach (arms stiff). Begin with 5 pound weight and work up to 15 pounds. Repeat 8 times.

        2. Pull-ups: Hands are reversed to develop biceps. Do a minimum of 10 and work for more. Develop arm strength, do not kick the feet.

        3. Bench Press: Begin with 45–50 pounds. Do the press 10 times for two sets. Repeat with 55 pounds, 60 pounds, and 65 pounds.

        4. Bent rowing: Lean forward, bending 90 degrees at the waist, lift bar from the floor to the chest, keeping the back parallel with the floor. Use the same weights and procedures as in the bench press.

        5. Isometric biceps press: For-hand and underhand, holding for 10 seconds with maximum exertion, repeat 3 times.

    B. Legs:

        1. Toe raises: Toes on 2 x 4 board, raising the heels, weights on shoulders (minimum of 55 pounds) repeating 10 times for two sets.

        2. Half squats (in a leg machine): Raise 75–110 pounds, repeat 10 times for two sets.

  3. Jumping rope: Five minutes, high and hard. Wear boots if they are available.

 C. Trunk:

  1. Abdominal board: Do 10–15 sit ups building to 25 times.

  2. Abdominal board: Twist at the top of each sit up, repeat 10 times.

  3. Trunk benders: Rotate the hips on a four count 10 times in each direction.

III. *Endurance conditioning.*

 A. Running stairs (twenty steps or more): Run 12–20 laps without using a railing.

 B. Wind sprints: Quick and hard the width of the gym, repeat 10 times.

 C. Over distance running: Run a mile as fast as possible without stopping.

Individual adjustments have to be made for each of these exercises. All adjustments should be upwards of these minimal requirements. The coach helps his players determine realistic conditioning goals.

Good physical conditioning is just the beginning of the program for victory. Winning seasons demand perseverance which ultimately leads to improvement. A team has to stick to their task over a long period of time. Staleness is a long time enemy of good performance.

COMBATTING STALENESS

All other factors being equal, a stale team is a loser and a fresh team is a winner. To keep fresh, individuals have to pace themselves for the long season. Several techniques can be employed by the coach to facilitate proper pacing for the long haul. These include:

 1. Progressively developing offensive and defensive systems.

Beginning with the simple and leading to the more complex.

2. Varying the practice schedule. Using different drills each day, changing player combinations, and breaking routine by changing the sequence of the practice schedule.

3. By using time efficiently. Avoid long, boring practice sessions. Practice sessions should never extend beyond two hours. There is a point of diminishing returns.

4. Filling practice sessions with learning situations that challenge the individual. As a season progresses learning should increase. Innovation is a stimulant to progress. Experimentation helps keep practice fresh and interesting. Later stages of a season should be used for extensive exploration.

5. Periodic breaks in practice scheduling are useful. Players will want to practice every day. At various intervals make all players take a day off.

The best way to eliminate staleness is to have a winning season. The pride a team takes in continuing to produce winning performances is the strongest deterrent to staleness. A fresh team has the best chance to "hang in there, all the way," persevering to victory!

BUILDING "CHARACTERS" OR CHARACTER BUILDING

The results of coaching are not always the same, and the variance is often caused by the motivation of the coaching. The coach can use his powers of persuasion in different directions. Some coaches choose to build the character of their players, while other coaches are busy producing "characters."

Character building is firmly rooted in respect. Players are dependent upon the coach for direction in learning to respect each other, the opponents, and the game officials. The coach is in a pivotal position to influence the attitudes of his players toward the entire game. He should direct his energy toward the development of mutual understanding. Players use respect to build constructive relationships with teammates. These relationships are characterized by a consideration of the welfare of the other person. A player who doesn't respect his teammates cannot be expected to respect his opponents either. The tragic results accrue to the individual, because by failing to respect others, an individual always diminishes his own character.

Respect for the rules of the game, and for the officials who enforce the rules, produces many intangible rewards. Players are keenly sensitive to the attitudes of the coach regarding the rules of the game and the officials who enforce them. Any hostility the coach expresses toward the officials will produce negative attitudes in his ballplayers. Coaches who disrespect officials can expect their players to use officiating to cover up for their personal mistakes. Meanwhile, the coach who is a gentleman honors the integrity of the game officials. He recognizes officiating as part of the game. Officials do not decide games; they administer them. Most officials are motivated by the desire to help boys grow through clean and honest game experience. Game officials represent authority. The coach or player who disrespects an official is challenging legal authority.

Many lessons for life are learned by players through competition. One important lesson should be the development of respect. Respect for teammates, for the opponent, and for game officials contributes to a general respect for all other forms of authority in society. The type of players who respect each other and the rules of the game are also the players who hold their coach in great esteem.

EFFECTIVE WAYS TO STALL

Stalling is effective when it uses up time without relinquishing ball possession and when it doesn't forfeit scoring opportunities. Stalling can be used for different purposes. The most common use of the stall is to make time pass in order to preserve a slim margin for victory. Other uses of the stall include efforts to secure the last shot prior to the time elapses at the quarters or at the half, to slow down the tempo of the game, or to freeze the ball when victory is assured in the fading seconds of a ball game.

In the final minutes of a game, it is important to distinguish between stalling and freezing the ball. The stall is used to slow down the tempo of the game. The ball and players are moved deliberately and cautiously, assuring the retention of ball possession; but they are continually scouting for opportunities to score the easy baskets.

The freeze is a total stall having the single purpose of maintaining ball possession while time passes away. The freeze is used when enough points have already been scored to win the game. The only possible way of losing the game would be for the offense to beat itself. Knowing the defense has the best chance to regain possession after missed shots, the offense freezes the ball. During a freeze, no player may take a shot, regardless of how easy the shot may be—*absolutely no shots are taken.* The freeze is only used when the offense has a slim lead, usually three to seven points, and there is less than a minute remaining. Under all other circumstances, it is best to use some type of stall. The stall emerges from the simple fact that the defense cannot score if the offense has the ball; and also every additional basket made by the lead team makes it more difficult for the opponent to win.

Several key principles should be followed when a team stalls:

1. All five players spread out on the court so that no one defensive player can guard two offensive men.
2. Keep the ball moving so that the defense cannot easily overload the ball.
3. Keep all players moving to make the defense play honest.
4. Players should break to open spots on the floor.

5. Make the easy and obvious pass whenever possible. Difficult passes lead to turn overs and the ball can be more easily intercepted.
6. Look for chances to score the easy basket (except during the freeze when no shots are to be taken).

Outside of these principles, the outstanding factor making the stall work is the poise of your team. The intense pressure of these moments calls for young men who make it seem like they have icewater in their veins. The composure of a team has to be maintained to execute the stall without flaw.

The lineup of the personnel in a stall may vary. I like to use a 2-1-2 spread design as shown in Diagram 8–1. If guard #1 has the ball, he has three easy pass options. He can pass to the opposite guard, to the strong side forward, or possibly to the pivot. Normally he should be inclined not to pass to the pivot, because the defense can collapse on the middle, putting double teaming pressure on the pivot. The open men are required to break toward the ball. If the strong side forward breaks free, the

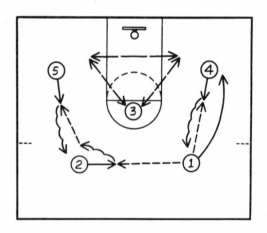

DIAGRAM 8–1
THE 2–1–2 STALL

ball is passed to him, and the guard breaks past him down the baseline looking for a possible return pass. The forward dribbles back out to the initial guard position. Notice that both the ball and players are moving. The stall pattern has evolved back to the original position, except that the forward and guard on one side of the court have exchanged positions.

The forward with the ball has the same options. Assume he passes to the opposite guard #2. Guard #2 dribbles the ball to his side of the court, while forward #3 and guard #1 assume their original positions. Guard #2 now has the same three options on the opposite side of the court. As these switches are taking place between the guards and forwards, the pivot man continues to break up and down the middle of the court. A good pass up the middle will produce an easy score whenever the pivot man frees himself under the basket. This sequence is simple to run, because what is really happening is that the forward and guards are swapping positions, filling the open spots on the floor as they switch.

TAKING FINAL INVENTORY OF YOUR PERFORMANCE

Final evaluation moves away from individual analysis toward group assessment. Evaluating the collective performance of your team is more difficult to accomplish because statistics are not as revealing for multiple execution sequences. Individual performances can be measured statistically in many different ways. Elaborate scoring ledgers have been developed to account for many different items including field goals attempted, field goals made, free shots attempted, free shots made, rebounds, turnovers, fumbles, fumbles recovered, and assists of different types. While all these measurements can be used to good advantage, individual statistics can be misleading if they are not related to collective performance.

It is possible for an individual to have an excellent set of credentials including good size, mobility, defensive agility, and scoring potential. The obvious conclusion would be that such a boy is a sure bet to help the team. The one outside factor which could deny him a spot in the lineup would be his failure to coordinate his abilities with the skills of other members of the team. It is not imperative for all players on a team to have equal ability. While the equalization of abilities may be an advantage for total offensive power, seldom do the component parts of a team match up evenly. More frequently individual team members can be differentiated by combinations of their skills, size, and experience.

Meshing the differing skills of team members into a single unified attack can be a difficult task. Collective evaluation is geared toward the assessment of relationship skills. The coach has to determine which combination of skills will produce the highest level of performance. To the amazement of some alumni and parents, this may mean changing the lineup in a seemingly contradictory way. The lineup can be strengthened by substituting one individual, who appears to be the logical choice because of his personal credentials, for another with less spectacular credentials, but he is willing to play with his teammates.

A coach has to make unpopular moves when he is convinced that the collective performance of a team will be increased by the change. The motivation for change is improvement. The results of a change should be measured by performance. While the improvement in performance may be easy to observe, it usually is very difficult to pinpoint the cause and effect relationships bringing the change about. It is almost impossible to prove collective performances statistically, because it is difficult to measure the effect which one player has on the others' performances. The final amount of productivity will be influenced by the coordination achieved by all the component parts of the offense. The offense will succeed to the extent that the offensive players are willing to cooperate with each other. Cooperating players complement each other in such a way that all the individual parts of the offense contribute—each member giving his best, some more and some less, but every part contributing to a united team attack.

Observation remains one of the finest tools of collective execution evaluation. In the past, coaches have used game films to study and re-evaluate group performances. I find video tape recording is less expensive and more manipulative. The video tape can be erased and reused many times, allowing coaches to tape practice sessions as well as the games. In this way coaches can focus attention on individual and group weaknesses by showing on video tape exactly what the problems look like. Seeing is believing, and believing creates incentive for the improvement and the cooperation necessary for a team to get capacity performance on offense.

CHAPTER SUMMARY

Basketball coaching is not measured by the quality of player personnel, it is determined by what a coach does with whatever material he has available.

The multiple offense gives the coach choice. After taking a complete inventory of his personnel, the coach determines which offensive strategy will best utilize the qualities of his team.

Winning coaches have a knack for taking charge. They control the tempo of the game by taking advantage of the opponent's weaknesses, and they force the opponent to play their game.

A winning team is always in top physical condition. Their preparation begins before the formal practice sessions by conditioning at home. Top physical conditioning has to be maintained during the season through supplemental exercises aimed at extending various muscle groups.

Evaluation is never complete in basketball. There is always room for improvement. Alert coaches never stop their search for the very best combination.

9

Attacking Zone Defenses
with a Simplified Multiple Offense

Many coaches contend they play the same offense regardless of the type of defense being employed against them. These coaches are of the opinion that a good man-to-man offense is also capable of beating zone defenses. While this strategy may work some of the time, I prefer to accept the challenge of the zone defense by planning a multiple attack; because the strategy employed by the man-to-man defense is basically different from zone defensing. Theoretically the offense should also be different in its attack. The primary differences of the man-for-man and zone defenses are easily recognized when we compare the basic tenets of each system.

The basic tenets of man-for-man defense are:

1. Each player is responsible for guarding one particular man.

2. The coach matches his players with the strengths of the opponent. Usually height against height, speed against speed, etc.

3. Each player watches his man first and then split-visions for the ball if possible.

The basic tenets for zone defensing are:

1. Each player is held responsible for a particular zone.
2. Multiple combinations are often used to team up on the strength of the opponent.
3. Each player watches the ball first, and split-visions to watch his man.

A complete offense should be capable of beating man-for-man defenses, any zone defense, or combination defenses. There isn't a single offensive design that has been developed to cope with every possible defensive combination. Coaches should be willing to modify their offense to meet the strategy of the particular defense they are playing against. Earlier chapters dealt extensively with man-for-man offense. This chapter focuses on zone offense. Each zone defense has unique strengths and weaknesses. By attacking the zone defense as an individual system, the coach is in a better position to fully exploit the weakness of the system being employed by the opponent.

SETTING UP THE OVERLOAD

In the zone defense, each individual player is assigned the guarding of any opponent in some particular area. The overload is designed to give any one defensive man more than he can handle by overloading a given territory with more than one offensive player. The overload is easy to set up, but difficult to defense. It can be set up from almost any type of basic alignment. We use either a 1-3-1 or 2-1-2 alignment, or slight variations of either. Overloads can be set up from either alignment. The 1-3-1 offense has built-in overloads formed by the natural triangles which are part of the basic design. Diagram 9–1 shows the various triangles formed against the defense. The baseline man #5 can move to either side forming new triangles with the wing man and the pivot man.

The 2-1-2 overload develops as either a forward or guard

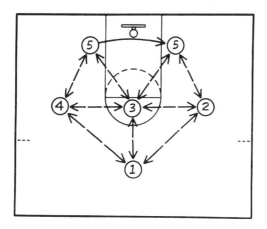

DIAGRAM 9–1
THE 1–3–1 OFFENSE

crosses court to overload a particular zone. Diagram 9–2A shows a forward overloading to the right side with the guards also shifting to the right. Diagram 9–2B shows the overload completed. If the defense fails to adjust, they will be outnumbered on the right side of the court. If they do compensate by sagging to the right side the offense can attack the weak side by reshifting or by using one-on-one clear-out techniques on the weak side. Of course, what is done to the right in Diagram 9–2 can also be executed to the left side.

MOVING THE BALL

Another important principle of zone offense is derived from the fact that the ball can be moved faster than individual players. This factor can be utilized to good advantage if the offense makes a concerted effort to pass short, quick passes evoking a defensive reaction. A zone defense failing to react to the movement of the ball is easy to beat. The strength of any zone defense

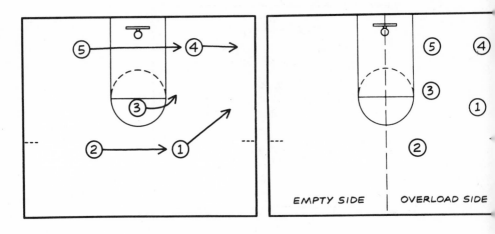

DIAGRAM 9–2A
FORWARD OVERLOAD

DIAGRAM 9–2B
OVERLOAD COMPLETED

is its ability to attack the ball. A moving target is always more difficult to hit. This rule also applies to a basketball. The faster the ball moves, the more difficult it is for the defense to control it. If the ball is moved fast enough, the offense will ultimately beat the defense simply because the ball can be moved faster than the defense will be able to adjust.

Passing is an essential part of zone offense. A sound rule for effective zone offense is to pass the ball whenever possible, dribble only when necessary. Passing is the element giving speed to ball movement.

MOVING PLAYERS AND POSITIONS

Motion is good for offense. Something moving is more difficult to stop. Just as it is good to move the ball, it is equally good to move your personnel. Naturally the movement must have purpose. Purpose relates closely to design. Motion can be designed to set up overloads, screens, and weak side shots.

Motions can be incorporated into almost any style of offense. The important factor is not *how* a team moves, but rather *that it moves!* Movement is not always easy against zone defenses because many zones are contrived to prohibit or, at least, to hinder movement.

The Follow-Through Maneuver

One very effective method of getting motion in the 1-3-1 offense is to incorporate the follow-through maneuver into the offense (see Diagram 9–3). Playmaker guard #1 passes the ball to the corner toward #2, who in turn passes it to the low pivot #5 who has come across the court from the weak side. Forward #2 moves through the defense to the opposite side of the court. The high pivot #3 drives behind the low pivot for a possible

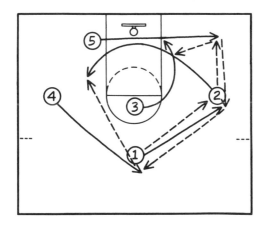

DIAGRAM 9–3
FOLLOW-THROUGH PATTERN

pass. If the pivot is not open to receive a pass, the ball is returned to the corner forward's position, which has been filled by the playmaker guard. Weak side corner forward #4 becomes the new playmaker guard. The ball is passed to him and he relays it to the weak side corner post which has been set by forward #2. In this sequence every player is in motion, as well as the ball. This makes the adjustment "double trouble" for the defense.

The Run-off Opportunity

Motion need not be complicated to be effective. While the follow-through pattern involves all five players in motion at one time, there are other less complicated patterns. The run-off opportunity, shown in Diagram 9–4, involves the playmaker guard passing to a wing man, blind screening his defensive man off onto the high pivot #3, and cutting low pivot for a return pass from the wing man. Now a triangle has been formed on the defense, creating an overload situation on the right side of the court.

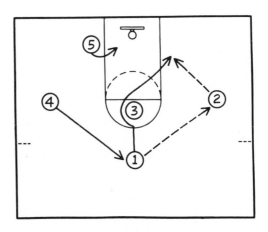

DIAGRAM 9–4
RUN-OFF OPPORTUNITY

The Run-off Opportunity with Post Exchange

If the run-off opportunity fails to produce a chance to score, it can be continued as shown in Diagram 9–5. The pattern continues with guard #1, who is now in the corner; passing to the low pivot who is freed by a screen set by the high pivot man. Contrary to common opinion, screens can be used against zone defenses. Screen the defensive man where he is and then allow the pattern to develop.

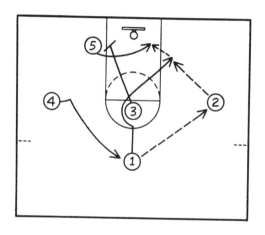

DIAGRAM 9–5
RUN-OFF OPPORTUNITY WITH POST EXCHANGE

CHANGING OFFENSES TO MEET PARTICULAR ZONE DEFENSES

Good coaching involves continual decision making. In baseball a manager strategically determines when to relieve pitchers. Football coaches are plagued with the decision to gamble for a first down or kick the ball. Similarly basketball coaches continually evaluate their offense to determine what offensive strategy will be the most effective. The opponent's strategy should affect your final decisions. Don't be threatened by the fear of making poor judgments. A coach who has never made a mistake has never really coached. Most often what is a good decision for one game situation, varies for other situations. So try something; if it works, repeat it again, and if it fails, try something different.

As a rule of thumb it is best to use the 1-3-1 (commonly called the Tandem Post offense) alignment against 2-1-2 zones and 2-3 zones, while the 2-1-2 offensive alignment works best against 3-2 zones and box zones. Adjustments are necessary for special zones. The fast break is also effective against most zones, particularly if the offense enjoys a height advantage.

As a change-of-pace we also use a Horseshoe Shuffle offense (Diagram 9–6) against zone defenses. This offense is a combination of the 1-3-1 and 2-1-2 offenses and involves a continuity sequence. The offense begins from a 1-2-2 alignment. Playmaker guard #1 passes the ball to guard #2 and breaks off the pivot,

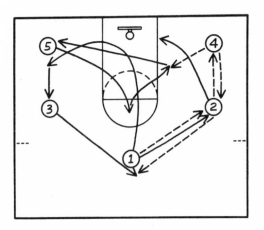

DIAGRAM 9–6
HORSESHOE SHUFFLE

which has been set by the weak side forward, and continues to the weak side. The ball moves to the corner pivot #4, with the guard driving the baseline. The ball can be passed to either the driving guard, the pivot who overloads the area, or back to the weak side guard who fills in the backcourt on the strong side. The whole pattern can then be repeated to the opposite side.

FORCING THE DEFENSE OUT OF THEIR ZONE

The best and quickest way to force a team out of their zone is to score. A hot shooting team will ruin any zone that is put to it. Chances for scoring against the zone are dramatically increased when a team moves the ball quickly and decisively. Once a player has freed himself for a good shot, he has to employ his skills to make the score. In the final analysis, shooting effectiveness will determine ultimate success or failure against the zone defense. The offensive system has to provide the high percentage shots while each individual works to get himself free. In this way the coach gets the good shots for his offense; the players have to make them. Zone defensive strategy is aimed at covering the ball, in preference to covering the individual man. Zone defense at its weakest point is vulnerable to open shots. If a player frees himself, and the offense is able to get the ball to him, he is in a good position to exploit the zone defense.

The confidence you have in your system will transfer to your players. Obviously, any lack of confidence is also communicated. This makes positive thinking imperative! The power of positive thinking in basketball is persuasive. Use it often!

CHAPTER SUMMARY

The principles of man-to-man defense and zone defense are different. Consequently, the principles of the offense used against these defenses should also vary.

The basic offensive strategy against the zone defense involves overloading specific areas on the court, moving the ball with quick, sharp passing, moving players, and rotating positions. The follow-through, the run-offs, and the post exchanges are patterns designed to accomplish effective motion on offense against zone defenses.

The best way to beat a zone defense is to shoot well. A hot shooting team will force the defense out of their zone.

10

Multiple Offensive Techniques
for Breaking the Press

Pressing defenses are here to stay. Any team planning to win their share of games had better take account of this fact in their preparation. There isn't another area in which weakness will be as apparent and devastating. My sympathy goes out to the team that isn't capable of handling a press. They will not only get beat; they will get beat bad! Losses of this type have a crushing effect on team morale. The confidence built up through many hours of work can be shattered in a moment.

Pressing defenses are intended to be disruptive. The basic elements that make a pressing defense effective are ruthless. Constant pressure, harassing tactics, total attack, quick transition, and complete floor coverage, combined with many unsettling individual tactics, are utilized to bring the worst out of the opponent. All this becomes depressing for the team that succumbs to the pressure of the defense; but don't be disillusioned. A team is only defeated when they think they are beat. A team that has faith in itself and in their offensive system, knows they are capable of meeting the challenge of the pressing defense.

This confidence, or lack of it, will often spell the difference between success and failure.

PSYCHOLOGICAL FACTORS

Confidence produces poise, poise elicits performance, and what results will either make or break the pressing defense. The team that lacks confidence, or begins to second guess its ability to meet a situation, is in real trouble against a pressing defense. Meanwhile, the team having confidence will be poised just at the moment they need it the most, resulting in the execution which will beat the defense. Repeated success against the pressing defense reinforces the confidence of the offense, enabling them not only to control the ball, but also giving them the chance to turn the press into scoring opportunities.

Fear produces a stigma that crushes confidence and hinders performance. Insecurity is the beginning of weakness. It robs the individual of dignity and leaves him the victim of intimidation. Failure is painful . . . and it is destructive. Pressing defenses have the capacity to shake a team badly. Individual and team weaknesses are nakedly exposed. This makes dealing with the threat of the press imperative.

CHECKING THE POTENTIAL TROUBLE SPOTS

Psychological readiness for dealing with the press involves both mental and physical preparedness. These factors are interdependent, and they begin with the individual. Mastering fundamentals is the beginning of certainty. The satisfaction of doing something right becomes the incentive for repeated performance. Confidence is developed over a period of time through a set of experiences. Confidence is never put on and off like a coat. The secret to success is knowing you have the capacity to do the job.

This internal certainty must be reinforced until the individual is convinced beyond a shadow of a doubt.

Breaking the press can be divided into three phases: the *entry,* the *advance,* and the *attack.* Problems can develop during any and all phases. Coaches having difficulty with the press should first identify the trouble spots, and then work out solutions to specific problems.

The entry involves getting the ball on the court and into play. It may sound easy, but it sure can be difficult; particularly when a team is pressing, and change of possession is imminent. Many pressing defenses aim at making the entry difficult while others allow the initial pass onto the court, and then double team the ball during the advance.

Advancing the ball upcourt causes the biggest problems for most teams. Usually the trouble is self-inflicted to a major degree. The most common error of the offense is to play into the hands of the defense by beating itself with poor ballhandling and inaccurate passing, leading to costly turnovers and eventual loss of ball possession. In contrast, a good ballhandling team will have the confidence and poise to advance the ball through the press for the attack.

The attack only becomes a problem when a team fails to adjust to the defense. Many times the offense has a choice during the attack to either fast break or to hold back and use their regular attack. Game conditions will dictate which alternative is the best. Teams prepared in all three phases of the press release should have little difficulty handling the press.

RELYING ON FUNDAMENTALS

When the going gets tough, the tough get going! This capacity to respond to game conditions is not inherent. It is the result of hard work and good planning. Natural ability, combined with arduous preparation and skillful application, produces winning performances. Offensive preparation for pressing defenses begins with the mastery of fundamentals. The mastery of all phases of ballhandling, including passing, dribbling, pivoting, and body control, contribute to the readiness of players to handle the press. Many different types of drills can be devised to simulate pressing conditions. The "Chicken Scramble" (Diagram 10–1) is a drill aimed at developing body control, peripheral vision, and dribbling skills. Designate an area approximately 15 feet by 30 feet on the court. We often use the free shot lane extended a few feet. Line up three groups on the baseline. Give a ball to the first two men in each group, for a total of six balls in the drill. On the sound of the coach's whistle, the first three men dribble to the opposite end of the arena, touching each sideline at least three times as they proceed, causing a zig-zag effect. When the first three men reach the opposite end, they pivot and return to the baseline in the same zig-zag fashion. As the first three men begin to return, the second three begin. Consequently, the drib-

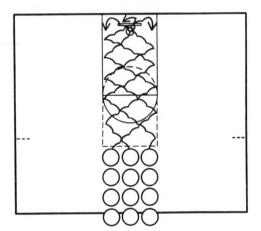

DIAGRAM 10–1
CHICKEN SCRAMBLE DRILL

As the first group begins to return, the second group follows the same zig-zag pattern up and back.

blers are forced to look up because the traffic gets fast and heavy. Watch for body control and make the dribblers look up, dribble low, and switch hands with change of direction.

The single most important factor in ballhandling is body control. There is a direct correlation between a player's ability to control his body and his ability to control the ball. Speed, change of pace, change of direction, and maneuverability are all affected by body control. Muscle tone, coordination, and physical conditioning all contribute to the attainment of body control. Therefore, all running drills, fast break drills, and agility drills are conducive to the development of body control.

One of my favorite agility drills that is aimed at developing body control is the 100% Drill. The drill is tough because it is a full court pressing drill. It places terrific demands on physical stamina and exerts precious influence on mental alertness. Players are paired into one-on-one groups of near-equal size and ability. One player assumes the offensive position while the other player applies full court pressure on defense. The offensive man is limited to only three dribbles in any one direction until midcourt. The defensive man makes continual effort to cut off the dribbling and passing lanes. At midcourt the offensive man pulls out all the stops. Hopefully, he will maneuver to beat his defensive man. If he does, the defensive man immediately pursues his man for possible recovery. In the process the offensive man gains valuable ballhandling experience against the pressing tactics of a man-for-man defense, while the defense also has the opportunity to refine basic man-for-man defensive fundamentals. At the opposite end of the court, the players exchange positions and return upcourt.

THE MAN-FOR-MAN PRESS RELEASE

A man-for-man press is only effective when every man on the court is covered. Loose men represent passing release opportunities that will break the press wide open. Offensive men who stand still are easily covered. Movement on offense creates problems for the defense. Entry is more difficult against the man-for-man press because most players are covered initially. To counteract the coverage of a man-for-man press, the offensive team lines up on the court in a 1-1-2-1 pattern as shown in Diagram 10–2. Guard #2 initiates the release by breaking to

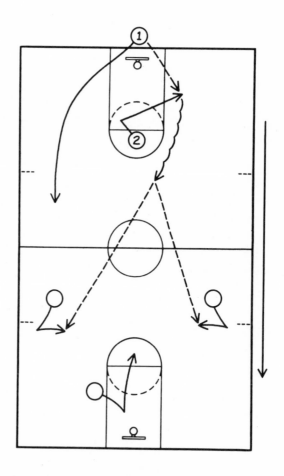

DIAGRAM 10–2
MAN-FOR-MAN PRESS RELEASE

either baseline. If possible guard #1 passes the ball to guard #2 and then breaks upcourt in the opposite direction for a potential return pass. The forwards always stay in the forecourt until they are needed. A good pair of guards should be able to handle the press by themselves. The forwards become a secondary release only when release guard #2 is completely covered.

Another alternative for getting quick entry is to use the full court lineup as shown in Diagram 10–3. All players line up down the center of the court and then spread to the positions shown in Diagram 10–2. The added movement resulting from the spreading technique often frees several men for a quick entry pass. The release continues as executed in the man-for-man press release.

The guard release action is very important to the success of the man-for-man press release. Primary reliance on the guards is by design. Keep the forwards in the frontcourt as much as possible. Each forward also draws a defensive man along with him. This added personnel in the backcourt will serve the defense more than the offense. The guards will be fully capable of handling the situation if they cooperate and play together. We spend many practice hours coordinating the play of the release guards against the press. The guards must learn to play far enough apart to spread the defense, but close enough together to pass to each other if necessary.

Overload drills make very effective press release practice. The Pressure Drill sets up a three-on-two overload situation on the guards. Designate two guards to take the ball up the court. Assign three defensive men to attack the two offensive guards. This situation will force the offensive guards to work at freeing themselves. Once the ball enters the court, the two guards are forced to play against the overload. This demands good individual reaction as well as coordinated effort between the two. It doesn't take long for the guards to realize that they should never abandon each other. With practice the guards develop respectives relating to moving the ball under pressure. Appropriate

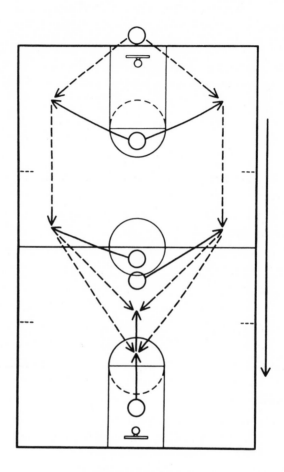

DIAGRAM 10–3
LINEUP RELEASE

individual reaction, combined with coordinated teamwork, will enable the guards to beat the press. The confidence they gain from this competitive practice should better equip them to handle similar game conditions.

THE ZONE PRESS RELEASE

A general principle the offense should follow, when operating against pressing defenses to advance the ball upcourt, is to primarily dribble against the man-for-man defense and to pass against the zone press. The teams attempting to dribble against the zone press will be susceptive to double-teaming traps. Most zone presses give the offense free entry of the ball onto the court. While covering the release guard, they double-team the ball as the advance begins. In this case the guards become dependent upon either the forwards or the pivot man for release.

Diagram 10–4 shows the defense in a 1-2-1-1 full court zone press (commonly called the Arrow Press). Free entry is allowed, but the ball is doubled-teamed immediately when it is received by guard #2. The weak side wing man covers guard #1. The forward release employs the use of either forward by breaking him into the frontcourt for a pass from the guard. The timing of the forwards break is crucial to the success of the release. The forward has several alternatives once he receives the ball. First, he looks to see if the pivot is open for a pass, he can return the ball to the guard who should have broken upcourt, pass to the opposite forward, or dribble upcourt.

The pivot release (Diagram 10–5) is effective against almost every zone press. It is also effective against the man-for-man press. The success of the pivot release is heavily dependent upon the abilities of the pivot man. He has to be physically coordinated and mentally alert to perform under pressure. If we have such a pivot, I rely heavily on the pivot release because a big man presents a good target for entry, and the advance upcourt is enhanced by his opportunities to pass to the guards. The forwards assume positions of readiness in the forecourt at the free throw lines extended. When the pivot man receives the ball,

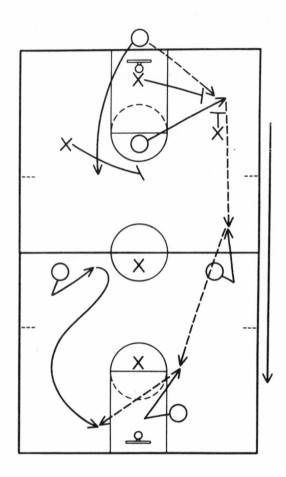

DIAGRAM 10–4
FORWARD RELEASE

he immediately looks upcourt for a possible pass to the forwards, which often leads to fast break opportunities. The diagram shows the pivot man lining up just beyond the midcourt line. As the zone defense begins to set a trap on the guards, the pivot man breaks into the backcourt as far as he has to in order to receive

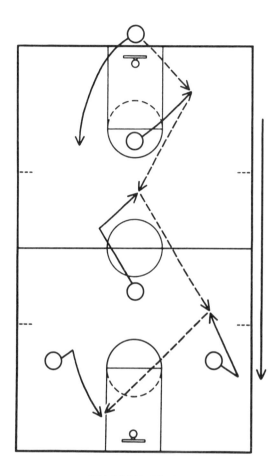

DIAGRAM 10–5
PIVOT RELEASE

the ball. When the pivot gets the ball, he has several alternatives to pursue. First, he should look upcourt to check the forwards for a potential pass upcourt, he can return the ball to either guard who have tail flipped around him, or he can dribble (only if he has to) upcourt.

TURNING THE PRESS RELEASE INTO A SCORING MECHANISM

The secret to breaking the press is to score against it. Once the offense begins to score, the defense is forced to abandon their press or lose. Press releases executed properly will provide appropriate entry and advance so that the attack can be applied to secure scores. The offense has the choice of making the attack part of the release; or if they are leading, they may choose to stall or use a more deliberate attack. In either case the defense is beat unless they can procure the ball. Any press release that keeps the ball moving upcourt, retains possession for the offense, and attacks for the score will eventually beat the pressing defense. The outstanding weakness of most press releases shows up in the form of a turnover, either as the result of poor ballhandling or muffed passes. To beat the press the offense must reduce turnovers and retain ball possession.

CHAPTER SUMMARY

The strategy of the pressing defense is clear. It is designed to harass the offense. Any sign of weakness on the part of an offense is sure to be exploited by a pressing defense. Effective offense is always launched from a position of strength. This position is attained when a team is ready both physically and mentally to execute their attack. Confidence is a product of successful execution.

The press release involves three phases: the entry, the advance, and the attack. A heavy reliance upon the mastery of fundamentals, including passing, dribbling, pivoting, and body control, is necessary to overcome the pressing defense.

Different types of press releases can be employed by the offense, depending upon the type of press being applied. The offense should be prepared to turn their press release into a scoring mechanism regardless of whether a man-for-man or zone press release is used. The offensive team capable of beating the press has garnered another weapon for its arsenal.

11

Preparing the Multiple Offense
for the Next Game

The work of a basketball coach is never finished. One game played and out of the way means another game is coming. Between games, time is short and work loads are heavy. Correcting the mistakes of the previous game, and making preparations for the next game, are a continuing part of the practice scene. Coaches are responsible for organizing practice sessions to make maximum use of both time and effort.

Planning Practice Sessions

Time is always a crucial factor in planning. Good planning saves time and eliminates wasted efforts. Short, but hard, practice sessions are more demanding, more interesting, and more productive. Long practice sessions tend to become boring and repetitive. The attention span of players diminishes as practice time lengthens.

Most practice sessions are scheduled at the end of the

school day. Coaches and players have usually put in a full day's work when practice begins. Therefore, practice sessions must be organized to recapture the interest and enthusiasm of all the participants.

ORGANIZING EACH PRACTICE WEEK

Assuming a game has been played on Friday, and the next game is on the next Friday, a typical weekly schedule would be as follows:

Friday: Game.

Saturday: Off.

Sunday: Off.

Monday: Moderate practice with emphasis on conditioning, error corrections, fundamentals, one-on-one play for offense and defense, and a brief skull session.

Tuesday: Hard practice, drilling fundamentals, drilling individual and team defense, preparing defense for Friday game again dummy offense, offensive set up, and scrimmage.

Wednesday: Hardest practice with emphasis on running, passing fundamentals, shooting, fastbreak, offense tuned against dummy defense, review of offense, addition of new plays, and hard scrimmage.

Thursday: Timing practice, very short (one hour maximum), emphasis on shooting, press release, jump balls, rebounding, final tuning of offense and defense, and climaxed by a brief and inspiring skull session.

Friday: Game!

ORGANIZING EACH PRACTICE DAY

Execution is learned during practice time by actually doing something. It matters little what a team does; it is more important that they are doing something. Good practice sessions simulate what has to be done to win ballgames. The more practice sessions resemble game conditions, the better they will be.

Practice sessions vary from day to day. It is difficult to predict specific practice schedule content far in advance, but it is possible to develop general guidelines. For comparative purposes, look at three, different daily practice schedules which detail a moderate practice, a hard practice, and a timing practice.

A Moderate Practice

3:30–3:45 Weight training, running a flight of stairs, and windsprints (150 ft.).

3:45–4:05 *Offensive fundamentals:*
Shooting—layups
Pivoting—four-corner pivot drill
Passing—four-corner hot box drill
Continuity Drill (combines dribbling, passing, and shooting): Wisconsin Criss-Cross drill.

4:05–4:15 *Rebounding:* Block out and release drill.

4:15–4:30 *Fast break drill:* four-on-two.

4:30–4:45 *Individual maneuvers:* one-on-one, baseline attack, and shooting.

4:45–4:55 Team defense or team offense (press release, applying the press, covering up on defense, and developing patterns).

4:55–5:00 *Endurance running:* 10–15 laps.

A Hard Practice

3:30–3:40 Conditioning (trunk benders, squat thrusts, set ups, isometric leg lifts, and weight lifting).

3:40–4:00 *Defensive footwork:* Thigh slapper, change of direction running, toughie defense, hands in the pants drill, and pursuit defense.

4:00–4:20 *Fundamentals:*
    Passing—hot potato drill, baseball pass drill.
    Shooting—layups, competitions shooting for seven (jump shots).
    Dribbling—Finger drill
    Coordination—Agility drill.

4:20–4:30 *Fast break:* the Blitz drill.

4:30–4:45 *Individual offense and defense:* the clear-out, the rocker step, rebounding, free shots, and baseline moves.

4:45–5:00 Set up team defense.

5:00–5:15 *Set up team offense:* Inside screen, outside screen, take two, the blind side, the pick, and specialty plays for the week.

5:15–5:25 Full court five-on-five scrimmage.

5:25–5:30 Windsprints.

A Timing Practice (Day prior to games)

3:30–3:35 Layups.

3:35–3:40 Passing drill.

3:40–3:45 Shooting.

3:45–3:50 Fast break drill.

3:50–3:55 Free shots.

3:55–4:00 Press release.

4:00–4:05 Stalling, out of bounds plays.

4:05–4:15 Final defensive tuning.

4:15–4:25 Final offensive tuning.

4:25–4:30 Free lance shooting.

4:30–4:35 *Skull session:* final instructions for coming game.

SCOUTING REPORTS KEEP COACHES INFORMED

Scouting reports are useful to the coach in two different ways: First, scouting reports help coaches become more familiar with the opponent's strengths and weaknesses; and secondly, they help the coach determine what strategy would be most effective for counter-attack. The information gathered from the scouting report should help the coach design game strategy that best exploits the opponent's strategy while securing maximum advantage for his own team.

Scouting reports seek answers to questions the coach is asking about his opponent. The following scouting report form asks short answer questions about the offense and defense of the opponent. There are four parts to this scouting report form.

A Four-Phase Scouting Report

PART I

Part I of the scouting report form deals with the collective execution of the opponent's defense and offense.

DEFENSIVE AND OFFENSIVE INFORMATION

_____ vs _____ Date _____

Defensive Information	Offensive Information
1. What type used? M to M, zone, or combination?	1. What is their main offensive threat? Fast break-set?

2. Do they usually switch on screen plays? When?

3. Where does their front line usually play? Sag or press?

4. Do they use a pressing defense?
   When?
   Where?
   How?

5. When does the defense pick up the guards?

6. Who covers the post? How do they play the post: front, side, or behind?

7. How do they line up on jump balls?

2. Are they free shooters, or do they play control ball?

3. Basic formation:
   3 in-2 out
   2 in-3 out
   2-1-2
   shuffle
   others

4. Players by position:
   RF
   LF
   C
   RG
   LG

5. Do they screen?
   Roll screens?
   Blind Screen?

6. Who are their best shooters?
   What type?
   From where?

7. Out of bounds plays:

BASIC DEFENSIVE PATTERNS

BASIC OFFENSIVE PATTERNS

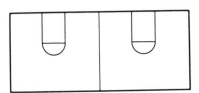

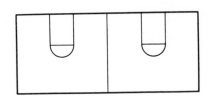

PART II

Part II is a team characteristic checklist. The answers to these short-answer questions provide a profile of the opponent's strategy both on offense and defense.

TEAM CHARACTERISTICS

                                        YES   NO

General

Is the team big?
Is the team fast?
Is the team aggressive?
Is the team in good condition?
Does the team have good competitive spirit?
Do the men fight hard for rebounds?
Are the reserves good?

Offensive

Does the team have an offensive pattern?
What type of offense is used?
Is the "post" used?
Where does the "post" man play?
How are passes made to the "post" man?
Does the "post" man shoot a lot?
Is it a good ball handling team?
Is the team deliberate?
Does the team use a fast break?
Do the men "cut" a lot?
Do the men use "give and goes"?
Do the men use "up and unders"?
Do men set up plays for teammates?
Do they use a sleeper?
Do the men shoot a lot?
Do the men take a lot of set shots?
Do the men take many one-handed shots?
Does he try to tap in rebounds?
Do the men dribble through a lot?

Defensive

What type of defense is used?
Does the defense withdraw?

Do the men get back to defensive positions fast?

Is a zone defense used?

Is an all-court press used?

Are set shooters given much room?

How is the post man played?

Do the men switch?

Are dribblers boxed out?

Do the men ball hawk?

Do the men slide well?

Do screens work on them?

Do the men turn their heads?

Do the men follow the flight of the ball on a shot?

Are they aggressive on defense?

Do they rebound well defensively?

PART III

Part III is an individual checklist of the opponent's player personnel. Space is provided to check the strengths and weaknesses of up to ten of the opponent's players. Usually a check of the starting lineup, along with the first-line substitutes, is adequate. This information is helpful in determining strategy both on offense and defense because coaches are in a better position to match players.

INDIVIDUAL CHARACTERISTICS

General

\# \# \# \# \# \# \# \# \# \#

Height

Weight

Is he is in good condition?

Is he a good team man?

Is he fast?

Is he a good rebounder?

Does he have good competitive spirit?

Offensive

Is he aggressive on offense?

Is he a good offensive man?

Is he a good dribbler?

Does he dribble through fast and hard?

Is he a good ball handler?

Is he a good passer?

Does he look to pass to cutting teammates?

Does he attempt "up and unders"?

Does he attempt "give and goes"?

Does he cut through hard and fast?

Is he a sleeper who does not get back?

Is he deceptive?

Does he change direction on cuts?

Does he try to bump his opponent into mates?

Does he screen for teammates?

Is he a good scorer?

Is he a good set shooter?

Does he take left-handed shots?

Does he take right-handed shots?

Does he shoot a lot?

Is he a good foul shooter?

Do they attempt to tap in rebounds?

Defensive

Is he aggressive on defense?

Is he a good defensive player?

Does he get back fast on defense?

Is he easily feinted out of position?

Does he turn his head on defense?

Does he watch the ball on a shot?

Does he switch well?

Does he fight hard for defensive rebounds?

Is he a ball hawk?

PART IV

Part IV is a worksheet that is used to make drawings of the offensive and defensive strategy used by the opponent.

PATTERN WORKSHEET

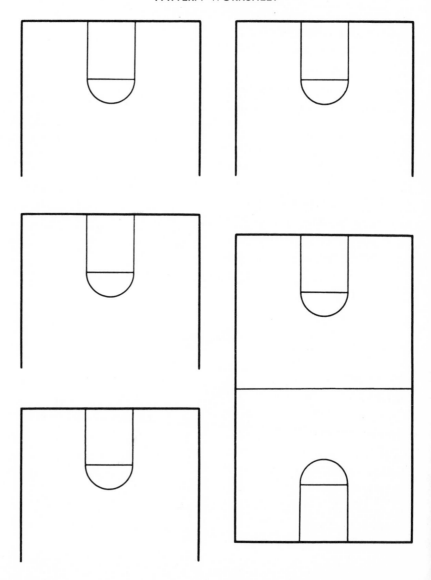

USING STATISTICS TO MEASURE PERFORMANCE

To maintain meaningful statistics a coach has to have a good statistician and a detailed ledger system. If you can find boys to register the statistics, I can supply you with an excellent source for a good ledger system. Lloyd A. Hinders of Rock Falls, Illinois has developed "The Comprehensive Basketball Scorer."* I have used it for ten years and find it to be the best scoring devise on the market. "The Comprehensive Scorer," a name that accurately describes its function, is complete because, while it scores the game, it also provides for a complete game summary. The game summary includes:

1. A game data sheet (illustrated on page 176).
2. A score sheet for both teams (only the "we" score sheet is illustrated on page 177).
3. An individual and squad accumulative record sheet (illustrated on page 178).
4. A multi-record sheet for each game to register violations, bad passes, fumbles, recoveries, held balls, and assists (illustrated on page 179).
5. An accumulative multi-record sheet (illustrated on page 180).
6. Quarterly shot charts for both teams (only first quarter illustrated on page 181).

"The Comprehensive Basketball Scorer" is designed to help the coach in several ways: 1) To give him a good "conventional box score." 2) To give a detailed record of statistics for each player for each game. 3) To give the coach an accumulative record of each player and the team as the season progresses. 4) Charts and record space are provided for every record a coach could want to keep.

---

* "The Comprehensive Basketball Scorer" can be ordered from Mr. Lloyd A. Hinders, 1005 Le Roy Avenue, Rock Falls, Illinois.

VS.

WE	OPPONENTS

WHERE PLAYED	DATE

REFEREE	UMPIRE

THIRD OFFICIAL	TIME OF GAME

SCORER	TIMER

SCORE: WE	SCORE: OPPONENTS

THE *Comprehensive* BASKETBALL SCORER

No. Quarters	Number	NAME	Personal Fouls	QUARTERS				Running Score
				1	2	3	4	
1 3 / 2 4			1 4 / 2 5 / 3 6					1 61 / 2 62 / 3 63
1 3 / 2 4			1 4 / 2 5 / 3 6					4 64 / 5 65 / 6 66 / 7 67
1 3 / 2 4			1 4 / 2 5 / 3 6					8 68 / 9 69 / 10 70 / 11 71
1 3 / 2 4			1 4 / 2 5 / 3 6					12 72 / 13 73 / 14 74 / 15 75
1 3 / 2 4			1 4 / 2 5 / 3 6					16 76 / 17 77 / 18 78 / 19 79
1 3 / 2 4			1 4 / 2 5 / 3 6					20 80 / 21 81 / 22 82 / 23 83
1 3 / 2 4			1 4 / 2 5 / 3 6					24 84 / 25 85 / 26 86 / 27 87
1 3 / 2 4			1 4 / 2 5 / 3 6					28 88 / 29 89 / 30 90 / 31 91
1 3 / 2 4			1 4 / 2 5 / 3 6					32 92 / 33 93 / 34 94 / 35 95
1 3 / 2 4			1 4 / 2 5 / 3 6					36 96 / 37 97 / 38 98 / 39 99
1 3 / 2 4			1 4 / 2 5 / 3 6					40 100 / 41 101 / 42 102 / 43 103
1 3 / 2 4			1 4 / 2 5 / 3 6					44 104 / 45 105 / 46 106 / 47 107
1 3 / 2 4			1 4 / 2 5 / 3 6					48 108 / 49 109 / 50 110 / 51 111
1 3 / 2 4			1 4 / 2 5 / 3 6					52 112 / 53 113 / 54 114 / 55 115
1 3 / 2 4			1 4 / 2 5 / 3 6					56 116 / 57 117 / 58 118 / 59 119 / 60 120

TIME OUT 1 2 3 4 5	TOTALS BY QUARTERS				FINAL

177

INDIVIDUAL AND SQUAD ACCUMULATIVE RECORD

NAME	NO.	F. G.			F. T.			P.F.	T.P.	Pt. Avg.	No. Qtr.	REB.		Assist
		Att.	Ma	Pct.	Ma.	Mi	Pct.					Off.	Def.	

MULTI-RECORDS — THIS GAME

NAME	NO.	Violation	Bad Pass	Fumble	Recovery	Held Ball	Assist
TOTALS: WE							
TOTALS: THEY							

179

MULTI-RECORDS — ACCUMULATIVE

NAME	NO.	Violation	Bad Pass	Fumble	Recovery	Held Ball	Assist
SQUAD TOTALS							
SQUAD AVG. PER GAME							
OPP. AVG. PER GAME							

SHOT CHART

WE
FIRST QUARTER

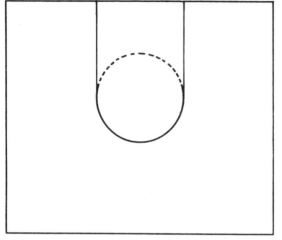

NO.	SA	SM	Pct.
—	—	—	—
—	—	—	—
—	—	—	—
—	—	—	—
—	—	—	—
—	—	—	—
—	—	—	—
—	—	—	—
—	—	—	—
—	—	—	—
—	—	—	—
—	—	—	—
—	—	—	—
—	—	—	—
—	—	—	—

TOTALS

THEY
FIRST QUARTER

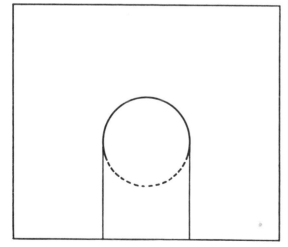

NO.	SA	SM	Pct.
—	—	—	—
—	—	—	—
—	—	—	—
—	—	—	—
—	—	—	—
—	—	—	—
—	—	—	—
—	—	—	—
—	—	—	—
—	—	—	—
—	—	—	—
—	—	—	—
—	—	—	—
—	—	—	—
—	—	—	—

TOTALS

181

In a looseleaf type of book, the coach can insert extra sheets to take care of the games over and above the 25 provided in the book. This enables the coach to keep the entire season's record at his fingertips in one volume. Charts can be removed and marked on a clipboard during the course of a game. The shot charts provide space for charting shots by quarters. The multi-record sheet provides for charting violations, bad passes, fumbles, recoveries, held balls, and assists. The diagram chart may be used to chart offensive and defensive rebounds, or for any other diagrams the coach may want to record.

CHAPTER SUMMARY

Planning practice sessions involves both daily and weekly scheduling. Planning eliminates waste and helps to capitalize on time. Each practice session should be designed to serve specific functions. A planned practice session simulates game conditions giving purpose to the practice schedule.

Scouting reports keep coaches informed. They should be aimed at identifying the opponent's strengths and weaknesses enabling the coach to prepare an appropriate counter-attack.

Statistics are used to measure performance. Present-day basketball coaching is a very scientific profession, and a coach needs to know all the "credits and debits" of his boys. By keeping records the coach will have a good statistical picture of his team as the season moves along.

12

Molding a Winning Combination

Many coaching responsibilities cannot be included in theory. A great number of coaching decisions are left to the better judgment of the coach. In these cases there is no substitute for experience, because the lessons of trial and error become the medium for problem solving. This gives part of coaching an arbitrary quality for which it is difficult to give specific guidelines. This chapter deals with many, different intangibles that fall into this arbitrary category. What follows in this chapter represents suggestions in the form of general guidelines which hopefully will help the coach make appropriate decisions. The application of this content should be modified by the person, the approach, and the goals of the individual coach.

INSTILLING PRIDE

Pride creates expectation, expectation stimulates enthusiasm, enthusiasm influences performance, and performance equals production. This progression illustrates the dynamic im-

pact pride has on performance. Instilling pride is a major task of
the coach. He will need the whole-hearted cooperation of every
ballplayer on the team. The total team effort should unfold something like this. We tried . . . we won . . . or we lost. A team
that tries, often wins; but if they lose the battle, they still have a
chance to win the war.

The concept "we tried" involves three important factors
which determine whether or not a team is genuinely doing their
very best. The first factor is physical conditioning. A team can
only reach full potential if it achieves top physical condition.
Any measure short of top flight conditioning is a form of cheat-
ing and will prevent the team from ever reaching full potential.
The second factor involves the total process of learning the
game, beginning with individual fundamentals and concluding
with precision team play. The third factor involves the development of wholesome mental attitudes toward self, others, and the
game. All these factors interacting simultaneously will determine
a team's ultimate degree of success.

The aim of coaching is to integrate these three factors into
the best combination possible. A good starting point is for the
coach to exemplify the goals he has set for his team. Human
beings are known to be great copiers. Naturally, ballplayers
copy their coaches either for the good or for the bad. Your
example may determine your players' attitudes. A coach who
takes pride, and tries on all three levels mentioned above, can
expect his players to imitate him.

COMMUNICATION IS ESSENTIAL

Sociologists tell us society is suffering from the consequences of various generation gaps. According to these men,
children are losing the respect for their parents, teachers fail to
understand their pupils, police officers misinterpret teenagers,
children resent authority, and barriers are developing between

many different groups in society. Coaches are in a good position to bridge the gap between the adult world and the teens. Communication becomes the vehicle that carries the messages between the team members and the coach.

Effective communication is always based on trust. A coach has to cultivate positive attitudes toward boys to secure their confidence. In like manner, players solicit trust by being persons of integrity. The consequence of this mutual understanding is the development of wholesome mental attitudes; however, the attainment of these attitudes is not without struggle. Coaches and players alike have to recognize and contend with three basic elements that affect communication. They are:

1. Recognizing the ego factors in athletics (getting);
2. Recognizing the team approach (giving);
3. Reading the messages completely and honestly.

Athletics in general, and basketball in particular, has been criticized because of the ego factors that are aroused by playing the game. Self-esteem, crowd approval (including parents, peers, and girl friends), self-challenges (such as point averages and defensive reputation), newspaper headlines, and thrill satisfaction are some of the ego-inflating factors most frequently cited. These factors are not necessarily negative, but they must be recognized in order to contend with them in a constructive way.

All of these ego factors stimulate competition. Competition does not have a moral quality in itself. It is the application that determines the quality of competition, and coaches are dealt the responsibility of using it with prudence. Used properly, competition becomes the basic tool of self-evaluation. Self-evaluation should be the primary goal of all coaching. It even takes precedence over winning. When players grow beyond the years of innocence, through adolescence, and into adulthood, they will recognize completely that getting something out of athletics is measured directly by what is given. What they will comprehend more thoroughly as adults, they must begin to experience as they grow to maturity.

The equation is simple and clear: Getting is equal to giving. *Getting* in basketball is primarily an individual matter, while *giving* has to be measured individually and collectively. The process of giving involves a transition from the singular "I" to the plural "We." In this manner individuals give and the team receives. The team concept emerges from the willingness of the entire squad to give every ounce of their physical and mental capacity so that the team will reach peak levels of performance. Only teams willing to pull together make it to the top. Communication is the key factor facilitating this pulling together. Reciprocal messages must be sent and received by players to players, by coach to players, and by players to coach.

Sending messages is easy, but reading them completely and honestly is more difficult. Solicited messages fall on willing and listening ears, while unsolicited messages often fall on deaf ears. Honesty is the measuring device determining what is heard.

Communication Devices

Straightforward talk is the most effective communication known by man. The freedom to say what is on our minds, assured that it will always be used constructively, is a healthy inducement toward building personal relationships. Next to his father, a coach should be a boy's best friend. While this friendship is not expressed in the same manner as are peer group relationships, and certainly does not compete with them, it does reflect a coach's genuine concern for the welfare of boys. The individual players should also develop concern for the welfare of one another. A mutual concern for the welfare of all team members should emerge out of these positive relationships.

The coach should continually open new avenues of contact between his players. The need for communication increases as the season grows longer. Personal involvement with individuals is the most effective means of communication, but other supplemental methods can also be employed. Some examples are:

1. *The Team Meeting:* Self-discipline is worthy of pursuit. Occasionally the team should meet under the leadership of the team captain without the coach present. The players are free to list any grievances they have against the coach or fellow teammates. Major problems not resolved by the group are referred to the coach by the captain.

2. *Skull Sessions:* Brain storming ideas are not born every day, but coaches do have messages to convey. These meetings should be short and meaningful. Their content should have application for immediate and future performance.

3. *Bulletin Boards:* To be used for announcement purposes, to distribute vital information, and to convey spirited messages of encouragement.

4. *Personal Notes:* Reserve the personal notes for special events. There are times when a coach has a message he wants clearly understood. Rather than impulsively verbalizing, the coach carefully formulates a personal note. Among other thing a personal note can be used to encourage individuals who are disappointed, to stimulate the entire team to new goals, to generate enthusiasm, to boost team morale, and possibly to point to specific games. The following is an example of such a note:

Memo to: All the Varsity Team Members
Re: The West Catholic game . . . and Winning!

Tonight we play West Catholic . . . many of our fans are looking past the Falcons to Friday night's game with Ottawa. These fans are well intentioned, but their attitude hurts. Fortunately there are many other fans who will be at the game tonight. They will help us get up for the game, but we should not depend on others to do a job that we can better do ourselves. Ask yourself what you have done to prepare yourself for the game tonight. Have you set a goal? Have you shared your feelings with fellow teammates?

We are striving to be No. 1. Being No. 1 takes guts, sacrifice, discipline, concentration, and most importantly application. We have a job to do tonight. Let's do it, and let's do it right. Vince Lombardi said it, and because I believe it, I am sharing it with you: "Winning is not a sometime thing, it's an all-the-time thing. Winning is a habit. Unfortunately, so is losing."

The game tonight might very well be won on the boards. West Catholic has the biggest front line in the city. I challenge you to outscrap them on the boards, to beat them on defense, and to outhustle them all over the court.

Best wishes for a great night at West Catholic.

Cordially,

Coach Bykerk

GOALS OF COMMUNICATION

It is amazing what can be accomplished if no one cares *who* gets the credit. Any team attaining this ideal has built a framework that will give them deep satisfaction along with many rewarding returns. Attainment always begins with seeking. Competition is the life blood of the game. Individuals begin by competing with themselves, extending competition to teammates, and conclude with a vigorous competition with the opponents. Competition works like a catalyst, producing change in performance. The individual continually strives to improve, but his accomplishment should never give rise to boasting.

The object of the game is to outscore the opponent. Every time your team wins a game, they have succeeded in meeting this objective. While winning is the primary objective of the game, there are other goals of equal and even greater significance. They include the development of teamwork; understanding individual roles and capacities; accepting defeat; value training; building strong physical bodies; attaining wholesome mental attitudes; encouraging spiritual growth and exchange; learning to share; and helping boys mature into young men through reflective experiences. While every team is not capable of producing a winning record, they are capable of attaining other equally important goals. Judging by these criteria, a team with a losing record can still have a successful season.

Coaches are fortunate to work with boys during their formative years. How fortunate this is for the boys depends largely upon the attitudes of the coach. Coaches are dealt responsibilities they cannot escape. Meeting these responsibilities demands positive attitudes toward young men. One of the strongest motivations for basketball coaching is the opportunity to use basketball as a means for bringing the best out of boys through vigorous and honest competition. Teaching meaningful applications will leave deep impressions on youthful minds. This makes learning in basketball much broader and deeper than just learning to shoot baskets. There are many lessons for life that should be underscored. These lessons have carryover value. Therefore, they can be practiced on and off the court. The single most important product of these lessons is *confidence*.

Confidence is the basic ingredient of success. Confidence grows as individuals develop self-acceptance, a feeling of security, self-reliance, the desire to accept others, actually accepting others, and accepting God. These concepts are interrelated—they have consequence for each other and one leads to the other. A person only begins to accept himself when he recognizes value in his own person. Self-acceptance is the beginning of security. To be loved, is to love. To have friends, is to be a friend. All these things become possible by faith, which is the essence of confidence; faith in the dignity of the individual, faith in the worth of fellow man, and faith in God.

A team that is working with these perspectives has many

advantages. They are in a good position to become successful, because confidence is a principal ingredient of success. Being right with themselves, with their teammates and with God allows a team to concentrate on other problems which are sure to confront them. The kinds of problems needing solutions are getting more complicated as dense urban populations continue to swell. Racial prejudice, breakdown of law and order, the hippie craze, the rise of public dissent, and societal pressures to conform threaten to demean society; and all these problems have serious implications for coaching in many areas of the country. While communications are often cold, calloused, and sometimes even non-existent in society, coaches must build personal relationships that cross many cultural and ethnic barriers. In days like these, coaches can make unusual leadership contributions.

COACHING SHOULD HAVE IMPLICATIONS FOR LIFE

Coaching distinguished by a purpose is exactly what the game of basketball needs. As I see it, the purpose for playing basketball extends beyond the game. The immediate goal of seeking satisfaction and experiencing ultimate success is enriched by teaching values which have implications for all of life. The significant quality of a purposeful life is usefulness.

Coaches are mighty useful people. They come with different styles and in every conceivable situation. In all cases coaching involves the helper and needy, the wise and seeking, the mature and immature, one who has lived the experience and one who hasn't. Helping others is a beautiful expression of usefulness.

Coaches looking for an example might give Jesus Christ a try. He has lived more deeply and profoundly than any other man. He can show us how to run with purpose and peace. Even in death He gave purpose to life. But to say He's a coach isn't saying enough. His death gives Him a unique dimension. Perhaps that's why you find His claim nowhere else in literature: "Come to me, all of you who are tired from carrying your heavy loads, and I will give you rest" (*Matthew* 11:28).

SETTING INDIVIDUAL AND TEAM GOALS

Individual and team goals should never be in conflict, but rather they should complement each other. In case of conflict, consideration for the team always takes priority over individual goals. Appropriate communication will minimize conflicts of interest. Players are sensitive to the coach's evaluation of the contribution they are making to the team. Players seek the coach's approval regardless of the level of their contribution; whether they are superstars, substitutes, or even managers. To the player, the coach's approval is synonymous with acceptance and disapproval is equal to rejection.

Each team member should set personal goals which take into account his range of skills in comparison to those of his teammates. The coach should assist his players by helping them set reasonable goals. Goals should reflect possibilities for improvement without sacrificing practical levels of achievement. There has to be a point at which challenges are fulfilled with accomplishment so that the player finds a reasonable level of acceptance. Taking account of the skills of teammates in setting individual goals is also important because variances in performance will appear as natural ability levels reveal themselves. Each player has to be encouraged to give his best. The final judgment as to who is doing the best has to be reserved exclusively for the coach. Players do not have to agree with the coach's judgments, but they *must* accept them until they can prove through performance, as judged by the coach, that they can do better.

The acceptance of the coach's judgment by all players is

crucial to the development of team goals. It is imperative for each player to understand his particular role on the team in relation to the contributions his fellow teammates are making. In this way every individual team member contributes his best so that team output will be at the highest possible level. Peak performances are only possible when players and team alike are motivated by *desire*.

PLAYING TO WIN

Winning teams have desire. They know it because they feel it, the fans know it because they can see it, and the opponent knows it because they are crushed by it. Desire cannot be hidden. It is written on faces, expressed in emotions, and displayed in performance. Teams playing with desire, play to the hilt. They never stop until the job is finished. In basketball, the task is not complete until you have made every effort to outscore the opponent. Play to win, and never be ashamed of it!

Winning teams play hardnose basketball. They keep their noses to the grindstone, making their own breaks and taking advantage of them, too. Hardnose teams don't like defeat. For this reason they practice with vengeance in preparation for winning performances. They work desperately hard, never seeking to escape, ceaselessly seeking refinement. When the stage is set, they are prepared to meet the challenge. Hardnose teams are comprised of fierce competitors. They have the desire to win; they have the will to win; they can sense it, feel it, and taste it. Hardnose teams compete to take the lead; once they get the lead they add to it, beating the opponent with certainty. In closely contested games the hardnose team executes to precision when it counts the most, turning the tide of the game to their advantage at the deciding moment. When the opponent is really tough, they bear down for their very best performance. If they lose, it will only be after they have expended themselves, giving every ounce of drive available. If they lose, it will be to another hardnose team that has all the same qualities except one—the winning team was superior.

THE "KILLER INSTINCT"

The "killer instinct" sounds inhumane. To avoid misunderstanding I will begin by defining what it is *not*. The killer instinct is not a destructive tool used to brutalize the opponent. It is not a device to be used for inflicting any form of physical or mental wound. It never gives a coach the license to profanity, or any other form of demeaning redress of either players or officials. The killer instinct refers to the need for clinching victory as soon as and whenever possible. Winning teams are opportunists. They capitalize on every opportunity to seize victory, realizing there is seldom a better time than the present to break a game wide open. Teams that pussy foot around with golden opportunities often end with defeat, losing games they could have won.

MAKING LOSSES PAY DIVIDENDS

If a team has exhausted every effort in the attempt to win, there is no shame in losing; but there will be disappointment. The level of disappointment relates directly to the margin of loss and the amount of effort expended. A team that tries little and loses by big scores, experiences little disappointment. Conversely, a team that expends itself; but looses by a close margin, will feel the sting of defeat. Hurt of this type becomes the incentive for correction and eventual improvement. Disappointment should not be feared; it is a lesson of life everyone should learn to interpret.

The converse of disappointment is satisfaction. The quality of disappointment is determined by the behavior that results. Individuals and teams feeling self-pity are abusively using their disappointment to a destructive end. Such a team or individual has chosen to be part of the problem rather than a solution to the problem. A more constructive choice would be for them to learn from their disappointment, recognizing the nature of the defeat, and pressing on to the formation of new goals. Positive confrontation leads to genuine satisfaction and growth.

Losing can be divisive. Losing is never popular with the fans. Sometimes it forces a wedge between the coach and resentful fans. A few short-sighted parents may also join the resentful crowd. Fortunately most parents are loyal and sympathetic fans. While fans are at liberty to give up on the coach, their divisiveness should not be allowed to infiltrate the player-coach relationships. Coaches can never afford to give up on their team. Players worth their salt respond by being loyal to their coach. Men of good character face up to defeat. They don't look for a crutch on which they can blame their loss. They seek each other with understanding and with hopes of building new inspiration.

Kids live in a dynamic world. What seems important one minute changes the next. A favorite escape route for young, inexperienced ballplayers is to forget the misery of the present by switching to the pleasantry of another activity. This diversion can be useful in helping the youngster adjust to the hurt of present disappointment, but it should never be used as a crutch to avoid reality. Confrontation is the best cure for disappointment because it elicits action. Action can be directed at solving the problems caused by the earlier defeat. Solving your team's problems, while creating new ones for the opponent, is the best way to assure victory in the future. Most teams eventually lose a game. The fact of losing is not as important as *how* a team loses. A dissatisfied team will convert their present loss into future wins. They make every loss pay handsome dividends by converting the present loss into greater margins of future success.

WHAT IS A BASKETBALL PLAYER?*

Between the innocence of infancy and the dignity of manhood, we find an unpredictable creature called a teenager. Some of them claim to be basketball players. Basketball players come in assorted weights, sizes, uniform colors and numbers, but all have the same creed: To play every game to the best of their ability.

Basketball players are found everywhere—in gyms, recreation centers, driveways, and alleys. Teammates kid them, officials anger them, fans cheer them, coaches criticize them, girl friends adore them, while mothers worry about them. And through it all they remain Spirit in a pair of tennis shoes, Dignity on a bench, Gentleness with their coach, and the best of young manhood with a ball in their hands.

When your team is behind, a basketball player is incompetent, careless, indecisive, lazy, uncoordinated, and useless. Just when your team threatens to turn the tide, he misses a layup, forgets to dribble, muffs a pass, fumbles the ball, fouls his man, or acts completely confused.

A good basketball player is a composite—he eats like a cow, sleeps like a lamb, but acts like a panther. To his father he has the speed of Ty Cobb, the moves of Bob Cousy, the brain of Einstein, and the shots of Bill Russell—all combined. To his coach he has the stability of mush, the speed of a snail, the mentality of a mule; and has about as much chance of playing the next game as would his own grandmother.

Meanwhile the coach is also analyzed. When his team is losing he is incompetent, uninformed, foolish, confused, too soft, and . . . unlucky. When his team begins to win, he is suddenly shrewd, hard-working, clever, careful, talented, and . . . lucky.

---

* "What is a basketball player?" is a parody of Alan Beck's famous piece of whimsey "What Is a Boy?"

His ability to teach is put on trial every time his team goes on the floor to play a game. He is a judge of talent if everyone's son plays all of the time.

A basketball player likes hot showers, high scores, long practice sessions, his name in the paper, and the satisfaction that comes from being part of a perfectly executed play. He is not much for windsprints, sitting on the bench, tetanus shots, picking up his towel, shuffle steps, or sarcasm from his coach about the girl's ring on his finger.

But all in all . . . a basketball player is a wonderful creature. You can criticize him, but you can't discourage him. You can defeat his team, but you can't make him quit. You can take him out of a game, but you can't take him out of basketball. He is a hard working, untiring, stubborn kid, doing the very best he can for his coach and his team. And when you leave the gym grouchy and upset because your team has lost, he can make you feel ashamed with just two sincerely spoken words—"WE TRIED."

WE DID IT . . . YOU CAN TOO

"We did it, we did it, we did it . . ." is the cry of the victor. The "we did it" philosophy marks the successful culmination of a genuine team effort. Put the emphasis where it belongs. *WE* did it! Yes, every single team member, including the managers, statisticians, and the coach. It was a collective goal that we set out to attain, and it is a team victory when accomplished.

During my years as a junior high coach, "we did it" many times by winning six league championships and one Mid-State Junior High Championship. Later as a junior varsity coach "we did it" by compiling a 17–1 won and lost record as we won the league championship.

As a high school varsity coach "we did it" in a very

spectacular way. For the success we achieved, I am deeply in-
debted to a group of hardnose kids who never quit. They were
the ones who made the impossible happen. Shortly after 1 P.M.
on March 19, 1966, 12,311 shocked basketball fans filed out of
Jenison Field House at Michigan State University in Lansing,
Michigan. The spectacular era of Detroit River Rouge as defend-
ing Class B State Champions had ended. King Rouge was dead!
They had strung together five straight state championships, winning nine Michigan titles in the previous eleven years. The impressive Rouge performance is a tribute to their coach Lofton
Green and his many fine teams. They had won 48 straight
tournament games without defeat. They were going after victory
number 49 and their sixth straight state championship. We
(Grand Rapids East Christian) were their opponents for the
final game.

East Christian was an unknown school in the tourney. East
Christian was a new school, having opened with two grades the
previous year. The first year we played without seniors, com-
pleting our regular season with a 10–8 won and lost record. It
was a real thrill to win our first district crown in our first year of
existence. We bowed out of the tourney in a thrilling 72–71
overtime loss to Whitehall in the regional semi-final game. It was
during the disappointment of this loss that we vowed we would
return the next year.

The next season proved to be an unforgettable experience.
We lost our season opener, a game we had no business losing;
but we knew we were beat fair and square. Fortunately we didn't
make the mistake of blaming each other. We lost together that
night, accepting the challenge of renewal. We continued our
season in mediocre fashion, finishing with a 6–6 record in our
City League and with an overall record of 10–8. After winning
the district championship in two close games, we entered one of
the toughest regionals in the state. In the regional final game, we
played Grand Rapids South Christian which had compiled a

22–0 record and earned the number 1 Class B ranking in the state. The final score was Grand Rapids East Christian 71— Grand Rapids South Christian 61.

On to State we went with our first would-be graduating class as loyal supporters. Our first two games at State were cliff-hangers, but we won both of them. Against River Rouge we were written off completely. It seemed clear to everyone, except our team, that the end of our road had been reached. To the general public there seemed to be no alternative other than to lose, but for our team another alternative was clear. Either we were going to be victim number 49 for the Rouge, or we would be the new Class B State Champions. The choice was easy to make. The task was difficult; but we tried . . . we won . . . we did it, we did it, we did it! The final score: East Christian 76—River Rouge 66.

The following year we made a desperate attempt to defend our State title. After repeating as district and regional champs, we beat undefeated and top-ranked South Haven in the State quarter final game. We lost to Detroit Willow Run 78–77 in the State semi-final game. We have not lost the vision of a possible return to the top. Winning the State Championship is every coach's dream. Have you ever dreamed of winning the state title? This is where it all begins. I know from experience. We did it, and so can YOU!

CHAPTER SUMMARY

A good basketball player takes genuine pride in his game. He works hard to master the fundamentals of the game and his enthusiasm has a good influence on his teammates. A few players excel. These players are competitive, communicative, and committed. They give 100% and their loyalty is beyond question. They realize that success is never final, and that defeat is never fatal.

Basketball is a rewarding game to play, but the future of basketball is dependent upon what the next generation is willing to give to the game. The game of basketball needs players and coaches alike who are willing to sacrifice for the future well-being of the game. The rewards of giving to each other and to the game will bring the satisfaction that accompanies completion.

Index